The Dynamics of
Salvation

The Dynamics of Salvation

Anthony F. Blessed Tarnue

"Until you are born again, you are not qualified for Heaven"

authorHOUSE®

AuthorHouse™
1663 Liberty Drive
Bloomington, IN 47403
www.authorhouse.com
Phone: 1-800-839-8640

Published by AuthorHouse 06/03/2015

ISBN: 978-1-4969-2170-3 (sc)
ISBN: 978-1-4969-2169-7 (e)

Print information available on the last page.

Author's e-mail address: tarnuea@yahoo.com
Telephone Number: (267) 844-6267

CONTENTS

DEDICATION

This book is dedicated to God Almighty for His enabling power.
I also want to honor the loving memory of my beloved parents,
Flomo and Malley Wuele, for their love and diligent care and
efforts in nurturing me into who I am today. Praise the Lord!

Special acknowledgements go to my beautiful wife Esther, and our children: Mary, Hannah, Vera, Harris, Love, Isaac, and little Loretta for their love and support. I am also grateful to Archbishop Joel Laurore and Mama Pastor Loretta Laurore, for training me in the school of the Spirit for 12 years.

To the dedicated and hardworking team from International Free Pentecostal Church (IFPC), Philadelphia, that spent sleepless nights editing this book as a service to God, and desire anonymity, I am deeply appreciative. To all our IFPC pastors, ministers, elders, deacons and members, thank you for your continued prayers and spiritual support.

PREFACE

It is said that among the many thousands of English words, the three most difficult are, "*I was wrong*," and the two most delightful are, "*check enclosed*." While this may be true, it can safely be concluded that the most dynamic word in any language for that matter is "*salvation*."

Salvation is dynamic for many reasons:

1. It connects heaven to earth by virtue of God's creation. The unseen world (heaven) created the seen world (earth). This makes heaven and earth inseparable because of the earth's total reliance on heaven for everything. Every blessing the earth needs to survive is a product of heaven, making heaven the savior of the earth.
2. It brings men back to God – salvation has created the grounds for sinful man to be able to return to God in fellowship and harmony.
3. It transforms evil to good – salvation uniquely turns darkness into light; drunkards into people of sobriety, and prostitutes into people of honor, integrity and peace.
4. It connects medical doctors, health care and other professionals to their patients, as it relates to their general health and wellbeing. God by His grace has raised these individuals as human saviors, thus bringing

marked improvements to the physical, mental, emotional and social state of millions of people worldwide.

Clearly, mankind faces a universal dilemma and judgment for sin. No continent, kingdom, nation, race, nationality or tribe is exempted. From creation to this day, Satan has always tried to wage a desperate, fierce battle against God and His creation.

And when we closely consider the spiritual condition of our One World, it is obvious that more than ever before, man's rebellion and sheer wickedness is multiplying due to the bondages of Satan. Unsaved mankind continues to reject the Lord, and the outcomes of such rejection are spiritual and physical deaths, coupled with moral decadence.

From the African perspective, the continent needs to be saved from heathenism (rejection of God), demonism, civil unrests, bloody tribal wars, immoralities, rampant corruption, non-patriotism, and extreme economic hardships.

It poses no question that similar problems and circumstances exist not only in Africa, but also in other under developed, developing, and developed countries. All continents and nations have problems that are unique to their own settings, and they have all led to the madness of spiritual, physical and material depravities.

Specifically, where does the Western world stand? As an illustration, let us look at the United States of America. While this nation may be considered the most powerful nation in the world, every aspect of spiritual, material and physical depravity has captured this multi-cultured and interracial society. Among these are apostasy (unbelief in God or rebellion), high divorce rate among Christians and non-Christians alike, dismantling of the family structure, immoralities, abuse of drugs and alcohol, materialism, as well as numerous other social, economic and political problems.

But from creation, it was not the plan of a loving God for mankind to live in such a disgraceful and demoralizing state. This is why even before creation, the plan and purpose of heaven was already laid out in the most loving, wonderful and amazing blueprint for the salvation of all mankind – the death, burial and resurrection of God's only begotten Son Jesus Christ, who would willingly become the One perfect sacrifice for the sins of every man, woman, boy and girl.

Accordingly, this book is intended to trace the root-cause of sin and examine the branches of salvation as they relate to the restoration of fallen man. While the book presents the Lord Jesus Christ, the Messiah to the unsaved, it also enlightens believers and encourages them to continue to live a life fully dedicated to God and the Christian faith.

Except otherwise indicated therein, all quotations and references have been extracted from the King James Version of the Holy Bible.

CHAPTER ONE

SIN: IT'S ORIGIN

A. The Creation of Adam and Eve

In the book of Genesis, we learn that Adam and Eve were the first humans created by the LORD God. They were created in the most perfect, sinless, and secured environment. God placed them in the beautiful self-contained Garden of Eden. Adam and Eve were both loved, blessed, and honored by God in every aspect of their lives (Genesis 1:26, 27, 31). In other words, their lives were whole and they lacked nothing.

"And God said, Let Us make man in our image, after Our likeness: and let them have dominion over the fish of the sea, and over the fowl of the air, and over the cattle, and overall the earth, and over every creeping thing that creepeth upon the earth" (v. 26).

"So God created man in His own image, in the image of God created He him: male and female created He them" (v. 27).

What is God's image in man? To understand this, we must first of all know that God's nature in man is two-fold:

1. His natural attributes
2. His moral attributes

1. The natural attributes of God are the internal qualities that define God as God:
   a) God is Omnipotent – He has all power; He is not limited by any circumstances, be it spiritual or physical.
   b) God is Omniscient – He knows everything. There is nothing on earth, in heaven, or in hell that is hidden from His holy eyes. He even knows the strand count of your hair (Matthew 10:30).
   c) God is Omnipresent – His presence is neither limited:
      i. By space, by wall, by earth, by heaven, nor by hell.
      ii. He can be everywhere or anywhere at the same time, unlike mortal man.
   d) God is eternal – He has no beginning or end.
   e) God is immortal – He has the ability to live forever.
   f) God is immutable – He is unchangeable in His being, in His Words, in His power and in His behavior (Malachi 3:6). His nature has no maturity development, nor growth and aging process.
2. The moral attributes of God comprise of holiness, righteousness, love, goodness, faithfulness, mercy, loving-kindness and compassion.

It is by reason of these qualities bearing fruit in the children of God due to our regeneration, that His image is fully manifested. This is explained more fully in chapter eight. So, when the Bible says God made Adam and Eve in His own image and likeness, the implication is that man is a product of God's natural and moral attributes.

Now, let's look at some of the reasons God referred to man as having been made in His own image. In this image, we know that Adam and Eve were living as king and queen in the Garden of Eden, on the basis of the Covenant relationship God had established with them. This Covenant was a conditional one, intended to seal their blessings, while ensuring their absolute obedience to the LORD (Genesis 1:28-30; 2:15-17).

Accordingly, the arrangement God instituted to guide the process Adam and Eve were to follow in their relationship to Him as well as to each other is referred to as the Dispensation of Innocence. The Bible describes six other Dispensations leading to the Dispensation of Grace. Generally, these Dispensations reveal in progression, God's interactions with all men over each period of time. And each time, mankind has utterly failed to live up to his responsibility to God. In the case of Adam and Eve, they were given the liberty to eat every fruit in the Garden except the Tree of the Knowledge of Good and Evil, or else they would surely die.

"And the LORD God commanded the man, saying, Of every tree of the garden thou mayest freely eat: But of the tree of the knowledge of good and evil, thou shalt not eat of it: for in the day that thou eatest thereof thou shalt surely die" (2:16, 17).

B. The Fall of Adam and Eve

The blissful state Adam and Eve enjoyed was soon to be cunningly intercepted by Satan, the deceiver and the accuser. He entangled Eve in a web of lies, deception and trickery against the LORD. Eventually, Eve convincingly yielded to him and ate of the fruit from the Tree of the Knowledge of Good and Evil that the LORD had forbid them not to eat (3:1- 6).

"And when the woman saw that the tree was good for food, and that it was pleasant to the eyes, and a tree to be desired to make one wise, she took of the fruit thereof, and did eat, ..." (v. 6).

Adam, in my opinion, was even guiltier of rebellion than his wife. He willingly, without hesitation, partook of the fruit from her hand. He gave no consideration to the fact that the command not to eat of the fruit was given directly to him, not to Eve. She listened to the serpent and was deceived, but Adam was not deceived; his act was deliberate.

Note that Satan's temptation was to charm Eve through her body (her flesh), soul (her immaterial self) and spirit (her willpower). Satan applies the same strategy today.

"... and gave also unto her husband with her; and he did eat"
(Genesis 3:6).

1. The results of the fall – Along with Adam and Eve, the entire human race was victimized by the fall. Sin is always a dreadful and catastrophic path for anyone to tread. Moreover, it has the natural tendency of badly affecting many other lives because no one can live independently. Your life is a network of connections to your family, friends and neighbors; your village, town or city; your state and nation and finally to the world at large. The sin committed by just two individuals in a concealed garden has now affected the entire globe (Romans 5:12). The practical lessons here must be seriously considered. It is only appropriate that whenever you are tempted, you must seek Godly wisdom in making all of life's decisions.

The glory of God, which was Adam and Eve's covering departed immediately, and they experienced a broken relationship with God their Father. God's glory is His tangible presence in the life of a born again

Christian. Have you ever experienced the presence of God in your life? In this sinful world, the presence of God is the most essential missing link in many lives. However, even though the sin of Adam and Eve temporarily disrupted that linkage, Jesus Christ, the last Adam, has mended it once again and restored our relationship with God (Matthew 1:23).

1. The curse – as a consequence of their sin, Adam the living soul, became Adam the dead soul: Adam's spirit, soul, and body were corrupted. His previously immortal body took on mortality – and he, his wife Eve and Satan received the judgment of the LORD God. The ground was also cursed:

    "Unto the woman He said, I will greatly multiply thy sorrow and thy conception; in sorrow thou shalt bring forth children; and thy desire shall be to thy husband, and he shall rule over thee. And unto Adam He said, Because thou hast hearkened unto the voice of thy wife, and hast eaten of the tree, of which I commanded thee, saying, Thou shalt not eat of it. Cursed is the ground for thy sake, in sorrow shalt thou eat of it all the days of thy life; Thorns also and thistles shall it bring forth to thee; and thou shalt eat the herb of the field; In the sweat of thy face shalt thou eat bread, till thou return unto the ground; for out of it wast thou taken: for dust thou art, and unto dust shalt thou return" (Genesis 3:16-19).

God our Father has never intended for any man or woman to come under a curse. His intentions towards us as His creatures have always been geared towards blessing us. This is clearly observed in the first chapter of Genesis. Everything that the Lord God created, He sealed by pronouncing a blessing upon them. Curses or punishments derive from the breaking of

God's laws, generally referred to as His spiritual laws. On the other hand, there also exists physical or natural laws, which we shall be discussing.

Spiritual laws apply to the spiritual world, and physical laws to the physical realm. It is essential to bear in mind that it was God that created both worlds. He controls the heavenly and earthly beings. Both worlds are connected to him and are subject to His authority. But let us first see what these worlds are made up of, and how they relate to all of God's creation.

1. The Spiritual world – this world consists of:
    a. The third heaven – according to II Corinthians 12:2, God's throne resides here. The Apostle Paul had a vision of this heavenly sphere.
    b. Abraham's bosom – in Luke 16:19-31, the Lord Jesus told a story about two men: One was wealthy and did not honor God nor man. The other called Lazarus, a beggar, esteemed the Lord highly. At the death of both men, Lazarus was taken into the bosom of Abraham, whereas the rich man was cast into hell – and there was a clear line of demarcation between the two places, rendering it impossible for any of them to travel from one destination to the other.
    c. The second heaven – this is illustrated in Ephesians 6:12, where Satan and his cohorts are described to be suspended in high places, practicing "spiritual wickedness."
    d. The Kingdom of God on the earth – this is comprised of all born again believers who have been translated from the kingdom of darkness into the kingdom of God and His dear Son Jesus Christ (Colossians 1:13).

As our High Priest, Christ has spoiled principalities and powers, ascended into heaven and is seated at His Father's right hand, executing His priestly ministry of intercession on our behalf. Believers here on earth are considered as living stones; a holy, royal priesthood (I Peter 2:5-9) and a kingdom of priests (Revelation 5:10). We have been clothed with the righteousness of Christ, to offer sacrifices of praise and thanksgiving; to offer ourselves as spiritual sacrifices unto Christ for His cause, and to reign in holiness and righteousness in a world in which we live, but yet are not a functional part thereof.

2. The physical world – it consists of the following:
    a. The kingdom of man on earth – this relates to the rule of man in all spheres of the physical world including: politics, education, arts, economics, music, technology and sports.
    b. The physical cosmos – (the cosmos itself is a complex and orderly system such as the universe). Physical cosmos may be composed of all physical phenomena within the first and second heavens that can be experienced through our five senses. Examples are the moon, sun and stars.
    c. The vegetable kingdom – this refers to the constitution or types of plants such as trees, vegetables, herbs, flowers, weeds and shrubs.
    d. The animal kingdom – this kingdom includes a composition of living organisms that comprise all animals.

As we can see, the entire world is an evidence of God's supernatural attributes, which far exceed the limited comprehension of the human mind. One thing that should be known by now is that God created both heavenly and earthly beings to honor, worship and serve Him.

1. Spiritual Laws – they apply to all of God's creation – angelic and human beings alike. They are intended to guide our actions. They lead us into a right relationship with God and man. Basically, they control everything that happens in the entire universe.

We know that Adam and Eve were to honor the LORD by reciprocating His love; communing and fellowshipping with Him; responsibly caring for the animal and plant life He had put in their charge; and most importantly, not eating of the Tree of the Knowledge of Good and Evil to avoid death. In other words, they were to believe in and obey Him. Belief and obedience sum up God's primary command to all His creation.

For their part, Moses and the children of Israel were commanded to have no other gods beside Jehovah, as written in the Ten Commandments (Exodus 20). This period was the Dispensation of Law.

Our forefathers in the Dispensation of Promise (Abraham, Isaac and Jacob), coupled with people throughout the rest of the Old and the New Testament eras, have been given God's Great Commandment: to love the LORD their God with all their hearts, with all their souls, with all their minds, with all their strength–and to love their neighbors as themselves (Deuteronomy 6:4, 5; Leviticus 19:18; Mark 12: 28-34; Matthew 22: 35-40; Luke 10:25-28).

So, when Adam and Eve violated God's law, they rightly deserved His righteous judgment; and they did suffer the just consequences for their offense.

By the same token, we remember how Lucifer or Satan was thrown out of heaven when he rebelled against God. You see, Lucifer (the "star of the morning,") was created as an angel, the anointed cherub, with the most astounding beauty. The Word of God in Ezekiel 28:1-19 further describes him as being of high perfection, blameless, and an accomplished musician with superior wisdom. As a cherub, his duty was to guide the throne of God; that is protecting the very holiness of the Most High.

It is almost unthinkable that with all the love and honor God bestowed upon Lucifer, he allowed the sin of pride to rule over him. Covered in unrighteousness, puffed up in vain glory, he believed he could viciously and cold heartedly dethrone the LORD (Isaiah 14:12 -14).

Please note that like Adam and Eve, Lucifer, too, had a choice to obey God's law or to run the exceeding high risk of disobeying Him and be cast out of heaven forever.

God continues to expect nothing less of His creation than total obedience. He demanded it of the Old Testament saints, and He demands and anticipates the same from the New Testament saints. Through the inspiration of the Holy Spirit, the New Testament sets forth several spiritual laws, so let's examine a few:

a. The law of faith – our great God Himself is the God of faith. He had complete confidence in Himself, that at His utterances, things would come into existence, and that is what occurred at creation.

It is faith that connects mankind to God. His Word says that all things are possible to them that believe. In order to know Him, you first have to exercise faith in Him and believe that He would save you (Ephesians 2:8; Hebrews 11:1-10).

Once a Christian, the law of faith maintains that you must continue to establish confidence in God and His Word, and not to doubt (James 1:5-8; Colossians 2:7; Hebrews 11:22).

b. The Law of sowing and reaping – this is one of the cardinal principles put forward in the Word of God. It works universally and applies to both believers and unbelievers. In Galatians 6:7 Paul states:

"Be not deceived, God is not mocked; for whatsoever a man soweth, that shall he also reap."

This means that everyone will be rewarded according to the path he/she chooses. If you plant the seeds of corruption, you will harvest the fruits of corruption, eventually leading to death and destruction (Romans 6:13; Proverbs 22:8). But if you sow the seeds of righteousness; of the Spirit of God, you will certainly be rewarded a life of righteousness, of the love of Jesus Christ and of Godly prosperity, all leading to life everlasting.

c. The law of sin and death – we have seen that this law was given by God from creation. It is still in effect. The law of sin and death emphasizes the fact that sin should not be taken for granted; its consequences are extremely severe because they result into spiritual and physical deaths, as well as eternal punishment (Deuteronomy 30:15; 19; Romans 6:22, 23; 7:1; 8:1, 2).

2. Physical/Natural Law – is a universal system of law that is determined by nature. It is also the use of reason to analyze human nature, which is the binding rule of moral behavior.
    a. Newton's Law of Universal Gravitation – this law describes the attractive gravitational force that exists between two objects. To put it simply, it is the force of gravity that pulls physical objects to the earth.
    b. The Rule of Natural Law with regard to Moral Behavior – this rule indicates that every human has a conscience and knows that behaviors such as drunkenness and theft are destructive to themselves and to society.

As spiritual beings and God's creation living in a physical world/ universe, we must allow the Spirit existing within us to lead us in positively impacting the physical world. If we walk in the Spirit, we will not fulfill the lusts of the flesh, but we will continuously make a difference in society for others to follow.

With all the scientific, academic and technological knowledge, our universe can never function effectively without the Creator, and certainly without us, the Body of Christ. The Spirit must lead the physical in order for the physical to succeed.

Beloved, your obedience to God's law is the path to your glorious destiny in life. If you want to obtain goodness all the days of your life, be careful to observe His laws.

C. The Restoration

"And I will put enmity between thee and the woman, and between thy seed and her seed; and it shall bruise thy head, and thou shalt bruise his heel" (3:15).

In spite of their sin and broken fellowship with the LORD, He released His first promise and assurance of salvation to them (and all mankind), through the coming of the Messiah.

1. The promise – God declared that Christ, by His death, resurrection and ascension, would take captivity captive, recapture power from Satan and relinquish that power back to believers. This was a written guarantee that there would be a lasting hostility between Satan and mankind. Yet, the LORD had a plan to save His creation and drastically deal with Satan. This means that although Satan would bruise the heel of Jesus by His death on the cross, Jesus would eventually have the victory through His resurrection and ascension. What a demonstration of His special grace and amazing love!

Indeed, God is love; His love is immeasurable, more than mortal men can imagine, more than they can understand. However, He is also the God that judges the unrepentant. Today, His Word reveals who He is in His natural and moral attributes. It speaks of His personality and character, and reveals all His innermost desires, plans and purpose for mankind.

2. Types/Foreshadows – Back in Adam's day when the LORD uttered His declaration in the account of 3:15 concerning His restoration of man back to Himself, He spoke in terms of *"types" (shadows, figures, or patterns)*. A *type* is described as an Old Testament person or thing that represents and pictures beforehand a person or thing in the New Testament Dispensation. Types could also refer to events, actions and objects. For example, we note that God used the coats of skins from an animal that He killed to cloth Adam and Eve before they were driven out of the Garden. The animal was a *type* of the bloody sacrifice of the *Antitype* – which looked forward to the coming sacrifice of Christ: *"Unto Adam and to his wife, did the Lord God make coats of skin and clothed them (Genesis 3:21)."*

a. The **Ark** – From their early existence up to the coming of Christ, God used *types* to teach Israel basic truths about salvation. We see God using the *"Ark"* (7:1, 7, 21) to save righteous Noah and his family from destruction. The *Ark* was, evidently, a *type* of Christ:

"And the LORD said unto Noah, come thou and all thy house into the ark; for thee have I seen righteous before Me in this generation" (v. 1).

"And Noah went in, and his sons, and his wife, and his sons' wives with him, into the ark, because of the waters of the flood" (v. 7).

"And all flesh died that moved upon the earth, both of fowl, and cattle, and of beast, and of creeping thing that creepeth upon the earth, and every man" (v. 21).

The LORD favored Noah and his family and secured them in the confines of the **Ark**. He then inflicted His fierce wrath upon the rest of the people, due to their failure to heed to His Word. God's call to them for repentance had, of course, fallen on ***deaf ears***. For about 120 years, He had waited patiently for their transformation, but they waxed even more in their outright rebellion. God's patience had finally run out, and they were all consumed by the waters of the flood. Since Christ's coming has been fulfilled, we use Old Testament *types* to present Him as the *Antitype* in the New Testament.

b. The bronze serpent on the pole that the LORD God commanded Moses to set up in the wilderness was another type of Christ (Numbers 21:5-9; John 3:14, 15).

"And Moses made a serpent of brass, and put it upon a pole, and it came to pass, that if a serpent had bitten any man, when he beheld the serpent of brass, he lived." (v. 9).

Israel as a nation refused to appreciate God Almighty for His wondrous works. They did not only murmur and complain against Moses, they also spoke against God and thus received His judgment. Unless we are grateful to God for His blessings, we could prevent Him from extending further blessings upon us. But let me point out that despite their rebellion, Israel was willing to repent and ask God's forgiveness through Moses, God's leader. They had to go through Moses because under the Mosaic Covenant, not everyone had access to God and to His voice.

3. Dispensation of Grace/New Covenant – we are already aware that Christ, our Messiah, is the only means of salvation. The New Covenant therefore rests on His sacrifice. He declares that He is the way, the truth and the life; no man can possibly come to God, but by Him.

Irrespective of the lengthy patience of God unto sinful man, now extending more than 2000 years since the manifested presence of Christ in the world, His grace should never be equated to leniency on His part – His genuine desire is for all to come to repentance. In II Peter 3:9, the Holy Ghost said: ***"The lord is not slack concerning his promise, as some men count slackness; but is longsuffering to usward, not willing that any should perish, but that all should come to repentance."***

In today's Dispensation, we can see that it is different. Romans 10:13 states:

"FOR WHOSOEVER SHALL CALL UPON THE NAME OF THE LORD SHALL BE SAVED."

God is no respecter of persons. When I was a child between the ages 9 and 11, living in my farming village in Liberia, West Africa, I prayed to the LORD in my native tongue to bring me to the "*white man's*" country, and God answered my prayer in His own time. The only distance between you and God is the Lord Jesus Christ.

When Israel made the request for Moses to pray for them he did, and the LORD God provided the prescription for their cure.

Friend, you will act like a fool if you refuse to follow God's prescription for your situation. Do not be like the fool described in Psalm 14:1 who proclaims in his heart that there is no God. The LORD's prescription did not fail the Israelites and it will not fail you. This remedy ensures the most perfect result in the manifestation of the presence of Jesus Christ the Messiah. Remember, He was the *shadow* or *type* to come. No matter how terrible the situation of the Israelites, their lives depended only upon their obedience. And so, under this *shadow*, all who obeyed God's voice through Moses lived.

This is a sure indication that no matter how sinful you may be, or how hopeless your situation seems, there is still hope for you. Today, God has made it very simple. You do not have to go to Jerusalem or Mecca to communicate with Him. If you will only lift up your heart to Him, accept what Jesus our Lord has done for you and call upon Him, you will receive His pardon: the Lord loves a penitent heart. In John 3:14, we have this promise:

> *"And as Moses lifted up the serpent in the wilderness, even so must the Son of man be lifted up:"*

There you have it – "*Look up to Christ and live!*" You don't have to die in your sins and go to hell. Until you are saved, you are not safe: ***"That whosoever believeth in him should not perish, but have everlasting life"*** (John 3: 15).

CHAPTER TWO

SALVATION: IT'S MEANING

A. General Terms

1. Salvation, as it Relates to Physical and Material Things

Salvation refers to a saving or being saved from danger, evil, difficulties, and destruction. Salvation denotes deliverance and preservation from evil. In other words, it is to be rescued and remain rescued from all kinds of madness of Satan, including adversities, ruination, danger or death. Salvation carries the idea of being freed or experiencing freedom from a physical disaster or pain of any sort. For example:

a) Israel, God's chosen people, experienced bondage and severe pain and suffering in Egypt for about 430 years. But that bondage was eventually broken, and the nation was set freed from their slave masters.

b) Peter, one of the first apostles of the New Testament Church, was arrested and jailed for about a week. He received his freedom when the Church prayed consistently for him (Acts 12:5-11).

c) Sometime during the approximate ten years of civil war in Liberia, West Africa, I was arrested by a rebel leader and placed in a make-shift jail. God released me when I lifted up my voice and prayed.

These and many other aspects of deliverance are examples of salvation from the natural standpoint.

2. Salvation, as it Relates to the Spiritual

a) Salvation, in this regard, is the spiritual and eternal deliverance of the spirit and the soul of man from Satan and all his contaminations.

b) It stands as the act of being delivered from the wrath of God destined to be executed upon the ungodly at the end of the age (Matthew 25: 41-46).

c) It is to possess the peace of God and to remain at peace with Him; that is, an act of reconciliation between God and man.

B. Salvation in Specific Terms, as it Relates to Fallen Man

1) Man's Viewpoint: What it is not

Individuals around the entire world who are not Christians do view salvation in various ways, ranging from their religious beliefs, to their cultural and traditional diversities. From my own cultural background, every young man and woman between the ages of 10 to 18 view salvation in terms of the boys being inducted into the so-called "*Porro*" society, and the girls into the "*Sande*" society.

Following the first two hours of "*initiation*," they are expected to remain in the "*bush school*" for about a year to be trained in the culture and tradition of their tribe. Upon completion and prior to returning to their villages, it is imperative that the young people abide by these procedures: Take a shower, put on new garments, take on new names, and relinquish all personal belongings they may have carried along. In the eyes of the "initiators" and the entire tribe, while the young people may have joined the "secret society" as "sinners," they were now coming out as "new persons" and "sinless."

According to Rev. Kenneth E. Hagin's book, "*Welcome to God's Family*," "the new birth/spiritual salvation is not confirmation, church membership; water baptism; and the taking of sacraments. According to the catholic doctrine, observing religious duties; an intellectual reception of Christianity; orthodoxy of faith; going to church, saying prayers; reading the Bible; being moral; being cultural or refined; doing good deeds, or giving money to the poor. The Lord Jesus said you must be born again" (John 3:3).

2) God's Viewpoint of Biblical Salvation

Biblical (spiritual) salvation is God *"giving birth"* to our *"human spirits."* When Adam was created by God Almighty from the dust, his body was dead. Not until God released His breath into Adam did he become alive! "**And the LORD God formed man of the dust of the ground, and breathed into his nostrils the breath of life; and man became a living soul**" (Genesis 2: 7).

At creation, Adam received two kinds of life from his Father – the spiritual and the physical. With the spiritual life, Adam was able to commune with God, and with the physical life he could relate to God's physical creation and to his environment.

Notwithstanding, when Adam sinned against God, his spirit-man, the spiritual aspect of his life died. This means that although Adam remained physically alive (up to 930 years), in the eyes of God he was dead. How? Because the life of his spirit which was responsible to relate to God had been cut off by the contamination of sin. And the Holy God cannot behold sin.

As a result of their fallen state, Adam and Eve brought forth Cain and Abel into this world, after their own *"likeness"* (Genesis 1:28). That process of procreation, however, completely differed from God's creative process in bringing both Adam and Eve into existence.

The difference is clear: the first couple was created in God's wisdom and in His way – in His likeness and image. Adam became alive by God breathing His precious breath into his nostrils. But their children were procreated in their own earthly, human understanding and freshly desires.

Thus, God's plan to renew mankind reestablished His life into man's spirit, soul and body. In short, spiritual salvation is the new birth. According to John 3:3-6, the new birth experience is by water and by the Spirit. It occurs in the below instances:

a) When God's Word is implanted into our hearts.
b) With the nature of God Almighty taking up residence in our spirits upon the reception of Jesus Christ into our hearts (John 1:12).
c) At the mystic union of God and man.
d) At the deliverance of our spirits from the corruption of Satan.

> *"Jesus answered and said unto him, Verily, verily I say unto thee, Except a man is born again, he cannot see the kingdom of God" (v. 3).*

> *"Nicodemus saith unto him, How can a man be born when he is old? Can he enter the second time into his mother's womb, and be born?" (v. 4).*

"Jesus answered, Verily, verily I say unto thee, Except a man be born of water and of the Spirit, he cannot enter into the kingdom of God" (v. 5).

"That which is born of the flesh is flesh and that which is born of the Spirit is spirit" (v. 6).

Since flesh can only give birth to flesh, the birth of the human spirit must be a supernatural act of God. This is a mystery and it is to be accepted by faith. When the supernatural becomes connected to the natural, the natural takes on the supernatural.

The Lord Jesus Christ in the book of Luke 4:18, 19 said:

"THE SPIRIT OF THE LORD IS UPON ME, BECAUSE HE HATH ANOINTED ME TO PREACH THE GOSPEL TO THE POOR; HE HATH SENT ME TO HEAL THE BROKENHEARTED, TO PREACH DELIVERANCE TO THE CAPTIVES, AND RECOVERING OF SIGHT TO THE BLIND, TO SET AT LIBERTY THEM THAT ARE BRUISED," (v. 18).

"TO PREACH THE ACCEPTABLE YEAR OF THE LORD" (v. 19).

Here are some other examples of salvation:

1) The healing of the broken-hearted: This means the healing of one's spirit and emotion. The heart, in scripture, refers to our spirit-man. This is not talking about our physical human hearts. It is the seat or center of the soul of man.

2) The deliverance of the captives: This aspect of salvation is the rescuing of our lives from our slave master, the enemy, Satan.

3) The recovery of one's sight: This could be both physical and spiritual, with reference to our enlightenment. When sin was imputed to the world, we lost our perception of God's holiness. Our hearts became darkened, and we experienced spiritual blindness. We also lost the wholeness of our human sight, creating the possibility of experiencing physical blindness. On the contrary, Jesus' birth ascribed unto us His salvation. He came to graciously place God's sight back into our hearts, thus restoring our spiritual and physical sights (John 5 and John 9).

4) Liberty to those Satan has totally crushed: Read Mark 5:1-21. The story is told of a man whose mental state seemed so deranged, that many regarded it as incurable. Being battled and bruised by Satan, this man lived in the cemetery. But when Jesus met him he was totally set freed from the dominion of Satan. His life and dignity were restored. Are you saved?

5) The coming of the Year of God's favor to His people (Luke 4:19): What was the Acceptable Year for them at that time, since the Lord Jesus was quoting from the Old Testament? According to Leviticus 25:8-13, this was the Year of Jubilee which means:

a. The time of great celebration and glorious jubilation.
b. The 50th year of Sabbath rest for all of Israel's lands.
c. The year of freedom and restoration of people and things:
   i. All mortgaged lands were returned to their original owners.
   ii. All farm lands rested from farming.
   iii. All slaves were released from slavery.
   iv. All family possessions were restored.
d. A year of remission of sins, or a time of forgiveness.
e. A time of new beginnings for every Jew.

In summary, this was the year in which two aspects of salvation were manifested. First, physical salvation – this carried the idea of rescuing all slaves from their masters, thus restoring their human dignity. Secondly, material salvation – a time of releasing the people's precious possessions which brought to them material wealth.

What does the Year of Jubilee mean to us under the New Covenant or Dispensation of Grace?

1) It is called the Day of Pentecost, meaning the fiftieth day after the Passover (Acts 2:1, 20:16).
2) It is also called the Feast of Wheat.
3) It marks the day on which the promise of the Holy Spirit came in a tangible way and visible form from God (Day of Pentecost).
4) This was the beginning of the apostolic Church in the New Testament.
5) It marked the glorious transformation of fishermen into missionaries of the Gospel message, great apostles, workers of signs and wonders, and magnificent orators who amazed the world.
6) This Dispensation of Grace is also known as the Year of God's Divine favor to His people; it has been made available to us today.

When the atonement of Jesus Christ is fully embraced by the sinful, the sick, the helpless and the needy, they become restored to life, health, holiness, power, and prosperity. They have the power to possess dominion over Satan and all of his cohorts. III John 2 explains it in this way:

"Beloved, I wish above all things that thou mayest prosper and be in health, even as thy soul prospereth."

CHAPTER THREE

THE "WHY" TO SALVATION

Why do all men need to be saved? There are three major reasons:

A. Spiritual depravity of mankind
B. Physical depravity of mankind
C. Material depravity of mankind

What does deprave mean? To be depraved means to be bad, evil, or ugly; to be corrupted, debased, immoral, twisted, or vicious. Being depraved is also to be degraded, perverse, or vitiate. It carries the idea of being unhealthy, degenerated and flagitious.

In other words, when Adam the man of God turned from God and united himself with Satan, every aspect of his life was contaminated with evil. Consequently, from possessing God's blessings, from being glorious, holy, spiritual, wealthy and healthy, Adam turned into this cursed, natural, sinful, poor and sickly individual.

Because of this, man in himself is ***no good*** (since the fall).

A. Spiritual Depravity of Mankind

1. Adam's Life Before the Fall:

a. Having been created in God's likeness and image (Genesis 1:26), Adam's life in this image was sinless. This means that his life was characterized by holiness, righteousness, and purity. This is the God kind of life. Adam at this point carried the nature of God in him. The LORD God was not ashamed to fellowship with Adam, and Adam was not afraid or ashamed to come into God's holy presence.

Let me inject a word of wisdom from my Archbishop Joel Laurore concerning the believer's true image in Christ: *"God's ability to make things happen... this is my image in Christ. God's power to create things...this is my image in Christ. God's fullness of wealth...this is my image in Christ...God's power... this is my image in Christ. God's holiness...this is also my glorious image in Christ."*

All these blessings are part of our redemptive package and heritage in Christ Jesus. In other words, God's image is **WEALTH** – therefore, our image in Christ is **WEALTH**! God's image is **POWER** – therefore, our image in Christ is **POWER**! God's image spells **VICTORY** – therefore, our image in Christ is **VICTORY**!

Apostle Laurore also indicated that, *"If you are truly born again you carry the genes of God inside you."* Thus **DEFEAT, POVERTY, SICKNESS AND DEATH** have no place in our lives, my dear friend. Thank God for this glorious revelation. That is also our image in Christ.

b. Adam was a carrier of God's glory. In Psalm 8:4, 5 we have this revelation through the Holy Ghost:

"What is man, that Thou art mindful of him? and the son of man, that Thou visitest him?" (v. 4)

"For Thou hast made him a little lower than the angels, and hast crowned him with glory and honor" (v. 5).

The glory of God, both in the Old and New Testaments, was nothing but the very presence of God Almighty. This was God's manifestation in the tangible form. By the LORD crowning Adam with His glory meant that from head to toes, Adam carried the presence of God.

When Moses the servant of God went before the LORD for forty days and forty nights, his face shown like a bright light as he returned to the congregation of Israel. Even the elders who stood before Moses marveled; they could not withstand his presence (Exodus 34:28-30).

"And when Aaron and all the children of Israel saw Moses, behold, the skin of his face shone; and they were afraid to come nigh him (v. 30).

How did Moses arrive at this level of glory? Moses had devoted himself to God and to the mission he had been called. As a mere human in the presence of the holy God, he had totally recognized his inadequacies and feebleness. His ardent desire to know the LORD better and to be established in His glory persuaded him to pursue God in obedience and meekness. Moses had experienced the greatness and power of the LORD, and he was depending only upon His help for success. The demonstration of this supreme level of the glory of God in his life brought him hope and gave him renewed supernatural courage, strength and endurance to continue the monumental task entrusted to him. Like St. Paul, Moses' example teaches us that our utmost desire as children of God must be to delight ourselves in Him so that truly, we can come to the riches of His glory. For the assurance of those very riches will bring the greatness of God's kingdom into our lives.

The life of Moses can be classified into three stages:

1. Moses, "the somebody" in Egypt – in Acts 7:22 the scripture says, ***"And Moses was learned in all the wisdom of the Egyptians, and was mighty in words and in deeds."*** For forty years all that Egypt had was deposited in him as a future prince. It took Moses personal discipline, hard studies and hard work to obtain this testimony. He committed himself to it; he had a "want to." Through the matchless grace and tender mercies of the LORD, you can achieve anything in life if you have the "want to." He will certainly lead you into the "how to."

2. Moses "the nobody" in the desert – to the extent that God in His divine providence controls everything in the universe, He always turns even our mistakes and failures into stepping stones to His divine destiny for our lives. When Moses lost his temperament and killed an Egyptian in defense of a Hebrew slave, he ran for his life in the desert, where he was forced to live another forty years. Just as he had lived in Egypt for four decades and had learned all the wisdom of Egypt, similarly, he had to painstakingly learn the wisdom of the desert. The providence of God was at work in Moses' life. I believe the God of his forefathers was preparing him to become the answer to the cry of his Hebrew brethren in Egypt. In this desert, Moses the former prince, became Moses the least. He underwent tremendous spiritual, economical, physical, emotional and social transformations – the desert represented a place neglected or abandoned; a place of solitude, loneliness or barrenness; a place of economic depravity; and unfavorable environment; a place that defied normal human sensibility.

3. It was only when the LORD God recognized that Egypt was completely out of Moses, that He called him and filled him with His glory for the

deliverance of Israel. And as Moses grew and matured in the LORD, His glory upon him was also magnified.

Friend, I say again that greatness in the kingdom is not a gift. It is costly; it requires your complete surrender and consistent endurance. Do you want to make a mark upon your generation? You can, if you have a "want to" being in the abiding presence of God. Begin now by receiving Jesus Christ as your Savior and Lord.

c.   Adam was created eternal and immortal before the fall. Adam was created to live eternally in the identical glory that he was crowned with by his heavenly Father. No form of death was allocated to him as long as he walked in obedience to God's Word. Genesis 2:16, 17 clearly state this fact:

"And the LORD God commanded the Man, saying, Of every tree of the garden thou mayest freely eat." (v. 16).

"But of the tree of the knowledge of good and evil, thou shalt not eat of it: for in the day that thou eatest thereof thou shall surely die" (v. 17).

d.   Adam was given dominion to rule and reign on the earth, like his Father God.

In Genesis 1:26b, we have these Words from the LORD God:

"… and let them have dominion over the fish of the sea, and over the fowl of the air, and over the cattle, and over all the earth, and over every creeping thing that creepeth upon the earth".

Adam was given such vitality of power from God that every creature on the earth was subject to him. Since that which is born of the spirit is spirit, we can rightly say that Adam was the god of this world (Psalm 82:6; John 10:34-36). If this is true, then why did the lives of Adam and Eve change so dramatically?

In Genesis 3:1-7, we observe Satan challenging God by his lies. He accused the LORD of failing to relay the whole truth. Satan was speaking in reference to the Word of God in 2:16, 17:

> "A*nd the serpent said unto the woman, Ye shall not surely die:*
>
> *For God doth know that in the day ye eat thereof, then your eyes shall be opened, and ye shall be as gods, knowing good and evil" (vv. 4-5).*

Here, Adam and Eve were presented with two choices: 1) to obey God's Word and live in eternal paradise or 2) to disobey God and live in the wilderness under the torture of Satan forever. In Deuteronomy 30:19 God said:

> *"I call heaven and earth to record this day against you, that I have set before you life and death, blessing and cursing: therefore choose life, that both thou and thy seed may live"* (v. 19).

Regrettably, Adam and Eve made the wrong choice; they took the wrong route, resulting into complete disaster. Friend, the decisions we make daily are powerful life or death choices. Life itself is full of choices. They can either build you up or destroy you. Adam and Eve's choice eventually pulled them down to their lowest level.

Today, many people are still suffering, not because God created them to suffer, but because of the wrong choices they have made and are continuing to make in life's journey. We who are already Christians have all it takes (the Word of God, the Holy Spirit, power, authority, knowledge and wisdom), to make right choices at all times. If, on the other hand, you have not been born again, I sincerely pray that right now, you will give your life to Christ. Surely, you don't ever have to be victimized by the enemy any longer. Your new life in Christ will endow you with His grace; it will afford you the ability to choose the right path in life. That is, the path of righteousness, so that you can enjoy the abundant life God has prepared for you.

At this point of degradation in their lives, Adam and Eve suffered the following depravations that we shall now examine:

2. Their Lives After the Fall

a. They immediately became disconnected from God. This is a comparison to what happens when a branch from a tree becomes disconnected from its vine – the consequences are always devastating:
    1. The supply line is completely cut off
    2. The branch no longer has any source of life
    3. It eventually withers and dies
    4. It becomes exposed to all kinds of dangers and contaminants

Here is the Lord's teaching regarding the above illustration from John 15: 6: "*If a man abides not in Me, he is cast forth as a branch, and is withered; and men gather them, and cast them into the fire, and they are burned.*" If you lose your sense of value on the earth, you become good for nothing. My hope for you dear friend, is that you'll never lose your value as a child of God, because value lost leads to lost morals.

When Adam separated himself from God, he lost his value and dignity on the earth. He became defenseless to all the attacks of the enemy. Note that to be disconnected from the LORD God, is to be lifeless. Every step pushes you back, away from God, and exposes you to death.

[Prayer] *"May every step you take bring you into the presence of God Almighty, in Jesus' name!"*

Adam's disconnection from God also opened him up to hardships or dangers. Therefore, Adam the great became Adam the small; Adam the ruler became Adam the slave; and Adam the blessed became Adam the cursed. He lost his authority to his enemy the thief or Satan (Luke 4: 5, 6):

"And the devil said unto him, all this power will I give Thee, and the glory of them: for that is delivered unto me; and to whomsoever I will I give it" (v. 6).

From the mouth of the thief, we gather that prior to Jesus' crucifixion, burial, resurrection, and ascension in glory, this thief had all powers on the earth.

The question then, is, who delivered such vast power to him, about which he could boldly brag? Was it God our Father? No, God forbid! From the account of Genesis chapters one and two, the power was delivered unto Adam by the LORD God of heaven and earth. According to God's proclamation and mandate, Adam was the sole recipient of it (Genesis 1:26, 28), but he lost this authority to Satan when he committed high treason against the LORD God. How? Adam accepted the words of the thief and rejected the Words of the Master, as we know.

Satan's authoritative rule over Adam and mankind finally ended when Jesus Christ the Second Adam appeared. He conquered Satan, disarmed him of the power and returned it to His Church (Colossians 2:15; Matthew 28:18-20). Praise the holy name of Jesus!

[Prayer]: *"Friend, In the name of Jesus Christ of Nazareth, we (I mean you and I) will never again lose our authority to the devil, Amen!"*

b. Adam and Eve's crown of glory left right away: *"**And the eyes of them both were opened, and they knew that they were naked; and they sewed fig leaves together, and made themselves aprons**"* (Genesis 3: 7).

When God's glory departed, Adam and his wife entered into a doom of darkness. From that instance, everything turned against them. They became spiritually bankrupted.

*"**Then Satan answered the LORD, and said, Doth Job fear God for naught?**"* (v. 9).

*"**Hast not Thou made a hedge about him, and about his house, and about all that he hath on every side? Thou hast blessed the work of his hands, and his substance is increased in the land**"* (v. 10).

These passages of Scriptures portray the fact that the devil himself was confident in his admission that indeed, he has no free access or authority to torment the believer. He does not hold the believer's life in his hands, as long as that person remains covered under the glory of God. Does this imply that Satan will not tempt the believer? No! Temptations will eminently come. However, as long as you do not embrace them, you will remain under God's covering and protection. In this secured environment, Satan's entrance into your territory is completely sealed. In order to continuously enjoy this security, you are admonished to refrain from habitual sins, and Satan will have no legal right to harass you. No matter which direction he comes, you will be safe on every side if you diligently and obediently walk with God. Look at the warning and promise from I John:

*"**My little children, these things write I unto you, that ye sin not. And if any man sin, we have an advocate with the Father, Jesus Christ the righteous: And he is the propitiation for our***

sins: and not for ours only, but also for the sins of the whole world" (2:1,2).

c. Their access to God's presence became limited. Take a look at Genesis 3:8:

"And they heard the voice of the LORD God walking in the garden in the cool of the day: and Adam and his wife hid themselves from the presence of the LORD God amongst the trees of the garden."

Can you imagine the abrupt and drastic changes that occurred in the overall personality of Adam and Eve? Whereas they would have once jubilated over the LORD's appearance in the Garden, they were now restless, exceedingly fearful and hiding from Him in shame and disgrace. Why? Because the glory that attracted them to God had departed, rendering them spiritually and physically naked. Henceforth, Adam and his wife could only speak to God from a distance. They had lost their spiritual perception and were no longer able to behold their Father's glory and holiness. No physical eyes can see God and continue to live, as mentioned in Exodus 33:18-20.

d. Adam and Eve both died spiritually. I believe Adam did not quite understand the true meaning of death simply because in his physical eyes, Eve did not immediately die after eating the forbidden fruit. So at her suggestion, he readily accepted her offer and ate the fruit. He failed to realize that he and his wife would first suffer spiritual death. But in addition to this, the Bible describes two other deaths. Let us proceed to distinguish them:

1. Spiritual death – This refers to man's separation from God on this earth. When Adam and Eve sinned, they were separated from God. Anyone who does not yet know Jesus Christ as Lord and Savior is spiritually dead as well. With regard to the unsaved who die without the Lord, they too suffer spiritual death and go to their father, the devil. God regards this death as the most significant. It serves both as the means and the conduit to hell.

2. Physical death – This is the separation of the soul from the body. Physically, the body becomes lifeless and is good for nothing, except to be buried. Everyone on the earth has an appointment with this kind of death as long as the Lord tarries.

Physical death is most critical for those who are not saved. It is important for you to be assured of eternal life with Christ before your human spirit departs this earth. Why not confess the Lord now and make it right with Him? This is all that matters! Please read Romans 10: 9, 10.

3. The most dangerous of all deaths is the second death, as described in Revelation 20: 15:

"And whosoever was not found written in the book of life was cast into the lake of fire" (v. 15).

This is God's prediction for those who refuse to obey. The lake of fire is their eternal doom. But there is still hope, according to John 3:16: *"For God so loved the world that he gave his only begotten son, that whosoever believeth in him shall not perish, but have everlasting life."*

As a result of God's love for you, He has already given many of you several years to prepare yourselves for His Kingdom. The Holy Spirit wants to remind us again about the love of the Lord in II Peter 3:9: *"The Lord is not slack concerning His promise, as some men count slackness; but is long suffering to us-ward, not willing that any should perish, but that all should come to repentance."*

Tomorrow is not guaranteed to any unbeliever; today is your day of salvation. The Lord is saying to you through His Word in Revelation 3:20:

> *"Behold, I stand at the door, and knock: if any man hear My voice, and open the door, I will come in to him, and will sup with him and he with Me."*

The most precious honor for God the Father is to take residence in you, through the representation of the Holy Spirit sent by His Son Jesus Christ.

e. Adam and Eve became slaves to the devil instead of masters. We have already pointed out that before the fall of man, Satan had absolutely no authority to rule over God's creation, to maintain dominance over Adam and Eve, to inflict them with sicknesses, pain, diseases, poverty and other forms of sufferings. All these curses came about as a result of man's rebellion to God's Word.

Because Adam's sin was transmitted to mankind, every unsaved person in the world today is being dominated by the devil, whether knowingly or unknowingly. Satan has blinded their minds; he has literally captured them in a web of trickery and slavery. In II Corinthians 4:4, we read these Words:

> *"In whom the god of this world hath blinded the minds of them which believe not, lest the light of the glorious gospel of Christ, who is the image of God, should shine unto them."*

Yes, the coming of the Lord has brought light into the world; no one has to ever remain in the darkness any longer. In Luke 4:18, Christ Himself declared:

"The Spirit of the Lord is upon Me, because He hath anointed Me to preach the gospel to the poor; He hath sent Me to heal the brokenhearted, to preach deliverance to the captives, and recovering of sight to the blind, to set at liberty them that are Bruised."

Friend, the day you have been awaiting is now here! The light you have been searching for is at this moment right there with you. Please do not miss the hour of your visitation. In every season in life, God has the habit of releasing special blessings for the benefit of His people. It is your prerogative to tap into those blessings, or allow them to slip by. Right now in this year 2015, God has released abundance of joy. This is our season of immeasurable joy. Paul the Apostle emphasized this in Philippians 4:4 when he said, *"Rejoice in the Lord alway: and again I say, Rejoice."*

[Prayer]: *I prophesy that you receive your spiritual sight right now in Jesus' name! May every blindness fall from your inner eyes right now, in Jesus' name, Amen!*

B. Physical Depravity of Mankind

From God's realm of creation, it is the spiritual world that created the physical. The life of the physical world is surely dependent upon that of the spiritual for survival. When Adam and Eve disconnected themselves from God's holy standards, their spirits and their physical bodies experienced death in many dimensions.

1. Their bodies became feeble and mal-functional. The physical energy they had once possessed before the fall was exhibited only because of

the glory of God in their lives. But they faced excessive weaknesses and incapabilities when the Spirit of God departed.

2. Adam's body experienced hardships (Genesis 3:19): *"In the sweat of thy face shalt thou eat bread, till thou return unto the ground; for out of it wast thou taken: for dust thou art, and unto dust shalt thou return."*

It's quite obvious that the measure of depletion of their physical strength and abilities would have been one of the contributing factors that led to their difficulty to fend for themselves at all levels of their existence. Sin is always costly, regardless of who commits it. Because of sin, Adam the dresser of God's Garden, became Adam the tiller of the ground. Sin made everything difficult for both him and his wife. As family head, whatever affected him also posed a direct bearing upon Eve.

3. Their bodies became vulnerable to sicknesses and diseases. In Deuteronomy 28:15, the LORD God said to Israel:

"But it shall come to pass, if thou wilt not hearken unto the voice of the LORD thy God, to observe to do all His commandments and his statues which I command thee this day; that all these curses shall come upon thee, and overtake thee:"

Before the fall, Adam and Eve did not encounter any ailment, affliction or infirmity. As a matter of fact, all of God's creation was engulfed by perfection – from His glorious inhabitants, to the plant and animal life, even to the earthly and heavenly environment – the LORD considered all He made to be pure and complete. But the moment Adam and Eve began to interact with the devil, they exposed themselves to sin and ultimate destruction. This means that sicknesses and diseases originated from them, as a result of their direct contact with God's enemy.

The discussion about sicknesses and diseases has become a controversial issue in our world. Some believe that these calamities derive from God. The firm view of others is the complete opposite: that from a Biblical perspective, God's record does not indicate that He created sicknesses and diseases, but that there are laws that govern His universe. And if they are broken, there are resultant consequences.

Here is something for you to remember. God is never the author of evil; it's totally against His pure and holy nature. If you were to ever yield to temptation and then begin to search for an answer as to whose responsibility it is, you ought to first eliminate the slightest possibility of the Lord's obligation. Instead, take a good look at yourself!

"Let no man say when he is tempted, I am tempted of God: for God cannot be tempted with evil, neither tempteth he any man:"(James 1: 13).

"But every man is tempted, when he is drawn away of his own lust, and enticed" (v. 14).

"Then when lust hath conceived, it bringeth forth sin: and sin, when it is finished, bringeth forth death" (v. 15).

Temptation in itself is not sin. It becomes sin when you do not resist it, but yield thereto. If you allow any temptation to advance to the stage of you yielding to it, then you have surrendered to lust. We are already aware of what the Scriptures indicate: that lust is sin.

Believers should not be enticed into yielding to any form of temptation. The lusts of the eyes and of the flesh, as well as the pride of life are all sinful cravings for physical pleasures, and for things that gratify self. They are the foolish pride people put in their so-called accomplishments and possessions. These are worldly desires that should not be so much as mentioned among believers (I John 2:16; I Corinthians 6:9, 10).

Eve, in her strong craving for that fruit, created a self-destruct avenue to fall when she yielded to Satan (Genesis 3:6). David, the most celebrated king of Israel; a man after God's own heart and a descendant of the Lord Jesus, also lusted when he failed to take his eyes off someone's wife (II Samuel 11:2-4; Exodus 20:14-17).

But the young man Joseph, instead of cowardly embracing sin, boldly ran away from his temptation to commit fornication with his master's wife, upon her request and insistence. His obedience to the LORD and his loyalty to Potiphar could not allow him to yield (Genesis 39:7-12).

The Lord Jesus Himself was tempted in the wilderness by Satan after fasting for 40 days and nights. Satan's endeavors at getting him to covet worldly things – food, power and wealth was useless. Christ remained steadfast in obedience to His Father and His Word (Matthew 4:1-11).

These general types of lusts are the tactics that the enemy will always deploy in order to win believers over, and sustain unbelievers in his wretched territory.

With the advancement of technology in our "modern" world, believers must be extremely dependent upon the Holy Spirit's help in keeping them away from the numerous temptations that accompany the uses of technological devices. They have a fair share of advantages and disadvantages. You must know the risks and avoid the temptations, especially when you think you are "alone" and no one is "watching."

In his wickedness, Satan has a subtle way of prompting you into many sinfully addictive acts. This warning is particularly for young people and immature Christians who are easy primary targets. The splendor, fascination, attraction and materialism are highly boosted by intense media advertisements in our society. These are lusts that bring only temporary happiness, not lasting joy and peace. In I John 2:15-17, the apostle John warns Christians not to love the world, neither the things it possesses.

4. Adam and Eve, by their disobedience, eventually brought upon themselves and the whole human race physical death Genesis 5:3-5:

"Wherefore, as by one man sin entered into the world, and death by sin; and so death passed upon all men, for that all have sinned:" (Romans 5:12).

Adam's eternity was reduced to numbers – from his state of immortality to that of mortality. When sin increased, the longevity of man was diminished from 900 years to approximately 120 years (Genesis 6:3):

"And the LORD said, "My spirit shall not always strive with man, for that he also is flesh: yet his days shall be an hundred and twenty years."

Despite this warning sin still multiplied, and man's duration on the earth decreased to the worst level – from 80 to 70 years (Psalm 90:10). But the good news is, your redemption has delivered you from spiritual death. You are now connected to our heavenly Father in all the fullness of His amazing blessings.

We have already established the fact that:

A. The devil is primarily responsible for sufferings and calamities upon mankind (John 10:10). He is also to be blamed for such a sharp reduction in man's longevity.
B. Man has a large role to play in contributing to the shortening of his own longevity on the earth. This is due to his sinful nature (Ecclesiastes 7:17):

"Be not overmuch wicked, neither be thou foolish: why shouldest thou die before thy time?"

Is it possible for one to die prematurely? The answer is yes! Adam died before the proper time (Genesis 5:5*).*

"And all the days that Adam lived were nine hundred and thirty years: and he died."

This was not God's original plan for Adam. At his creation, the LORD did not place any specific limitation on the number of years Adam and Eve could live on the earth. It was Adam who imposed the limitation when he sinned. As noted, the LORD God warned Adam about what not to eat so as to ensure that he would live forever (Genesis 2:17).

If eating the forbidden fruit could result into death, then Adam and Eve's obedience to God's law would have forever sealed their lives. But because of their disobedience, sin has increased throughout all generations – from Adam to Noah; Noah to Abraham; Abraham to Israel and today, to the entire world (Genesis 6:6):

"And it repented the LORD that He had made man on the earth, and it grieved Him at His heart."

By now, it is quite understandable that premature death came as a result of the multiplication of sin, having started with Adam and Eve.

C. Unbelief, doubt, fear and murmurings (Numbers 13: 31-33; 14:1-4. 26-29). These are the four major sins that God cannot put up with:

1. Unbelief vs. faith – the foundation of the Christian faith begins right here. God Himself calls unbelief evil. You cannot move God, touch God, or please God without faith.
2. Doubt – to doubt the existence and the power of God is to deny the Lord's help. The Lord Jesus did not accomplish any mighty work in

His home town of Nazareth because the Nazarenes did not believe in Him.

3. Murmurings – God hates the sin of murmuring. It hinders Christian growth, prosperity, peace and harmony.

4. Fear – there are different kinds including:
   - The fear of the Lord
   - The fear of evil
   - The fear of man

a. The fear of the Lord – is a positive reverence for God that makes you hate what God hates and love what He loves. In relationship to you as His creature, you fear God by not taking His presence and His Word lightly. If you fear God, you will not sin deliberately, that is, whenever you want to.

b. The fear of evil – this is the combination of all that Satan is. Although there might be people who do not believe in the existence of an entity called Satan, that does not rule out the fact of the existence of the devil. Infirmities, the outbreak of wars, earthquakes, tornadoes and deaths are all examples of some of the worst forms of evil that pose tremendous fear.

When it comes to the believer who is under the covering of Christ, his situation is different. He is no longer subjected to the torments and fears of any of these things. His hope is in the Lord as His great protector.

b. The fear of men – those who are feared by men clearly present a danger and threat to the tranquility and stability of society: all transgressors of the moral laws of God and society, a majority of whom include sociopaths, deviants, antagonists and egoists. They have professionalized crime and have desperately taken it to a new level, especially in this technological age.

Despite their unusual and offensive disposition, we must appreciate the fact that God has gracefully extended His love and mercy to them. If you are one of those, I pray with all my heart that you will grasp the depth of the wisdom of the Lord and accept His salvation free of charge.

The Bible teaches that obtaining the fear of the Lord is actually a precondition to gaining His wisdom. The 8th chapter of Proverbs explains that the fruit of wisdom is better than silver and gold; that wisdom leads one in the way of righteousness and in the path of judgment; that those that love it shall inherit the substance, and that their treasures will be filled.

This is to say that to fear the Lord is to hate evil, but to accept the truth of the Word of God. As a child of God, this places you in the honored position to fully benefit from His supernatural wisdom in living life to the fullest, in accordance with His divine will.

Here is a bird eye's view of the analysis of fear:

1. Who and what not to fear:
   a. Do not fear man (Matthew 10:26-31)
   b. Do not fear false gods such as agents of the devil, witches and voodoo men who claim to be gods (Judges 6:10 and I Samuel 17:32-36).
   c. Do not fear the reproach of man (Isaiah 51:7, 8).
   d. Do not fear fear (Proverbs 3:25,26)
   e. Do not fear death (Hebrew 2:14, 15)

2. Who and what to fear

   a. Fear God and honor Him with every fiber of your being (Leviticus 19:14 and Matthew 10:28).
   b. Fear God's name. Do not take His name in vain (Exodus 20:7).
   c. Fear your parents; honor and obey them (Leviticus 19: 3).

d. Fear hell – you fear hell by avoiding evil, sin and Satan (Proverbs 1:26, 27, 33).

3. The great benefits in fearing the Lord.
   a. You increase your level of wisdom (Proverbs 1:7).
   b. You prolong your years and days on earth (Proverbs 14:27).
   c. You attract divine satisfaction and divine protection (Proverbs 19:24).
   d. You add riches and honor to your life (Proverbs 22:4).
   e. You provoke prosperity, power and victory over your enemies (Ecclesiastes 8:12 and Isaiah 33:6).

D. The Tongue – Your tongue is a very powerful instrument. In Proverbs 18:21, God's Word has this to say about the power of the tongue:

"Death and life are in the power of the tongue: and they that love it shall eat the fruit thereof."

In Numbers 14:28, we discover that when the majority of God's people (the Israelites) used their tongues negatively, they prevented the blessings of God upon their lives, and this caused their untimely deaths (Numbers 14:28):

"Say unto them, As truly as I live, saith the LORD, as ye have spoken in mine ears, so will I do to you:" (v. 28).

In using your tongue as a believer, the lessons are clear: keep your tongue teamed, and cease all negative confessions against yourself and others. Remember that whatever you speak against the LORD God, you are actually speaking against yourself.

E. Misuse or abuse of one's body. Here is a short story about a man from my home town:

This man began to get very ill, due to alcoholism. He was eventually hospitalized and treated for this addiction. Upon recuperating the doctor said to him, "Now that you are well, do not drink any more alcohol, and you will prolong your life." But the man responded, "If alcohol will kill me let it kill me; but I will not stop drinking it!"

Without a doubt, you can guess what occurred. The alcohol did kill this man. Dear friend, if you do not apply a wholesome attitude towards life in general, you may reduce your life span upon this earth. However, this is not God's best plan for you. The LORD God desires a long, healthy and vibrant life for each of His children. He wants us to have the best quality of life, thus ensuring our satisfaction and prosperity. Praise the name of Jesus!

Here are some glorious promises from the LORD Himself about our longevity on the face of the earth, provided we observe His laws:

"And the LORD will take away from thee all sickness, and will put none of the evil diseases of Egypt, which thou knowest, upon thee; but will lay them upon all them that hate thee" (Deuteronomy 7:15).

Many men have made promises to God and to others. Unfortunately, they have failed to fulfill them, for one reason or the other, whether justifiably or not. The integrity our God possesses is of the highest quality, incomparable to any mortal man's. All His promises to us are *"Yea and Amen,"* in Christ Jesus. For there is no condition on the earth, in the heavens, or even in hell that could ever prevent the LORD God from fulfilling His promises to us. The Bible says, *"…for with God all things are possible"* (Mark 10:27).

Take a look at some living proofs of God's faithfulness to His Word:

1. *"So Abraham prayed unto God: and God healed Abimelech, and his wife, and his maidservants; and they bear children"* (Genesis 20:17).
2. *"And the Lord hearkened to Hezekiah, and healed the people"* (II Chronicles 30:20).

Here are some testimonies of God's faithfulness as well:

a. A lady in Liberia. This woman was so ill that she was bed ridden. The Lord told me to pray for her, and when my friends and I prayed a prayer of faith on her behalf, she was healed instantly. She jumped out of the house shouting, "Thank you Jesus, thank you Jesus."
b. I, along with some brethren from our ministry in the City of Zorzor, Liberia, offered prayers for an extremely ill child whose parents, relatives and neighbors had all given up for dead. The child's life was immediately restored after the prayers.

It is a fact that I and others have been used by the Lord on many other occasions and in similar situations. The praise and glory belong to Christ Jesus. I'm confident that by His grace, and as long as He tarries, His will and purpose for humanity and for our ministry and calling shall be manifested.

Let us now discover what the New Testament has to say about God's faithfulness. We are aware that part of the redemptive work of the Lord Jesus is the restoration of our physical bodies to perfect health. This was prophesied by Isaiah in chapter fifty three, verses four and five of his book, long before Christ's coming:

"Surely He hath borne our griefs, and carried our sorrows: yet we did esteem him stricken, smitten of God, and afflicted. But

He was wounded for our transgressions, He was bruised for our iniquities: the chastisement of our peace was upon Him; and with his stripes we are healed."

Because of all the sacrifices Christ made for you and me, I can now gladly and boldly confess that no longer are sicknesses, sorrows and grief my portion, in Jesus' mighty name. What about you? According to Matthew 8:17, *"That it might be fulfilled which was spoken through Isaiah the prophet, saying, HIMSELF TOOK OUR INFIRMITIES, AND BARE OUR SICKNESSES."*

How many of our sicknesses and diseases were taken away from us? All of them, including those in existence and those in the future. Christians can be assured of both spiritual and physical healing in order to live the most wholesome, fruitful and productive lives. Praise His holy name forever more!

C. Material Depravity of Mankind

From the account of Genesis chapters 1 and 2, we did indicate prior how exceedingly blessed Adam and Eve were before the fall, such that they lacked nothing, whether spiritual, physical or material. However, just as they were stripped of their spiritual and physical blessings, so it was with their material riches or wealth. Having lost all spiritual connections to the Lord, Adam and Eve were driven out of the Garden and dispossessed of all tangible wealth (physical and material). Their sin, of course, only rendered them liable to multiple problems and adversities. I think they lived in constant fear, always looking over their shoulders because they had lost the security of the sheltered Garden. Their lives were now encumbered with worries, stress and anxiety in the process of striving to eke out an honest living. Outside of the Garden meant a daily struggle to survive in the world – survival for them and their growing family. Food, shelter and clothing were basic necessities of life, the things they previously had no need to think about prior to the fall. The LORD had cursed Adam to the effect that by his sweat he would eat bread. For Adam and Eve, these words became a daily reality.

What a change in lifestyle; a general disruption in a once highly esteemed and blessed life. Adam's life had made a reversed turn from a glorious position of trust and kingship, to a position of distrust and slavery – likewise Eve (Genesis 3: 22-24).

Let us earnestly appreciate God who has not left us to the devastation of the enemy. The undeserved grace of Christ has rescued us from the bondages that previously entangled and connected us to this and every other depravity of Adam. Galatians 3:13, 14 explain this divine truth:

> *"Christ hath redeemed us from the curse of the law, being made a curse for us: for it is written, CURSED IS EVERY ONE THAT HANGETH ON A TREE: That the blessing of Abraham might come on the Gentiles through Jesus Christ; that we might receive the promise of the Spirit through faith."*

Beloved, God's plan and eternal purpose for all men is based on His foreknowledge, worked out even before the foundations of the earth. It was fashioned in advance of Adam's creation and his fall. It was a plan made by the deep wisdom and power of an Omnipotent and Omniscient God. This means that the total redemption of your spirit, soul and body was paid for long before you were even formed in your mother's womb; prior to your physical birth into this sinful world.

If you have not experienced the new birth, you really need to confess your sins right now to the Lord Jesus Christ, turn your life over to Him, and He will save you. Our dear heavenly Father has made all the necessary provisions for our salvation. You are indeed worthy of this great sacrifice of love.

CHAPTER FOUR

THE "WHO" TO SALVATION: WHO CAN BE SAVED?

Let me re-emphasize that salvation is the most precious gift that God Almighty has graciously bestowed upon mankind, through His Son Jesus Christ. It plays the greatest role in bringing mankind back to God. Nevertheless, God freely offers to every man, woman, boy and girl the power of choice. The exercise of our willpower to freely choose our own destiny is a unique privilege in His Theocratic government. It gives mankind the freedom to make personal life or death decisions. Let us remember that as much as it is the earnest desire and plan of the Lord for all men everywhere to know Him, His strategy does not coerce or force anyone. Individuals who come to Him must do so with willingness and whole heartedness. Eternity with Christ depends on denying yourself and choosing the path of Christ. Who then can be saved?

A. All can be saved (I Timothy 2:1-4):

"I exhort therefore, that, first of all, supplications, prayers, intercessions, and giving of thanks, be made for all men; for kings, and for all that are in authority; that we may lead a quiet

and peaceable life in all godliness and honesty. This is good and acceptable in the sight of God our Savior; who will have all men to be saved, and come unto the knowledge of the truth."

If God wants all men to be saved, it means that some men are not saved. Do you know the difference between the saved and the unsaved? Saved men and women are those whose sins have been washed away by the blood of Jesus. They have experienced a change in their lives. When you see them, there are obvious differences in how they walk, speak and behave, as compared to those who are not saved. If you have experienced the new life that Christ offers, you don't belong to yourself any longer; you belong to Jesus. You will love people, care for them and bring the lost to Jesus. We have this confirmed in II Peter 3:9:

"The Lord is not slack concerning His promise, as some men count slackness; but is longsuffering to us-ward, not willing that any should perish, but that all should come to repentance."

Let us take a careful look at this verse:

1. "The Lord is not slack concerning His promise, as some men count slackness" – this means the Lord does not think or behave like men do. God is never negligent concerning the things He has promised. He will never be, because His thoughts and ways cannot be compared to ours – they are higher, perfect and just. To conclude that God is slow is equal to robbing Him of His vital attributes of being Omniscient, Omnipotent and Omnipresent. In His sovereignty and faithfulness, God will always fulfill His promises to you and me.
2. "But is longsuffering to us-ward" – this means that God is exceedingly patient towards humanity. This degree of patience comes along with

compassion, kindness, mercy, consideration, with His amazing grace at the crown of them all.

3. "Not willing that any should perish" – if you are not born again, you are included in the "any." The word "perish" is something that you will never want to experience. From God's viewpoint, to "perish" means to be doomed forever in everlasting darkness, completely separated from His eternal presence. This is not God's plan for you.

4. "But that all should come to repentance" – repentance is the key word here. It means to change from Satan to God, from yourself to Christ, from sin to righteousness and from hatred to love. Are you willing to make this transition?

Beloved, God wants you and your entire family, circle of friends, community and nation to be saved. If you are already a believer, I pray that with urgency, boldness, and utterance, His Holy Spirit guides you in witnessing Christ to them.

B. The World Can be Saved

What is the world comprised of? It consists of all nations, kingdoms, and people that make up its general human population. The world has diversities of religious beliefs, cultural differences, and political and social ideologies and preferences. Christ came for the whole world because all of humanity is in need of salvation. Why? The answer to this question relates to the rapid increase of sin on a worldwide scale. Take a look at John 3:16, 17 and hear what our Captain of love says.

> *"For God so loved the world, that He gave His only begotten Son, that whosoever believeth in Him should not perish, but have everlasting life. For God sent not His Son into the world to condemn the world; but that the world through Him might be saved."*

Another supportive scripture is also found in (John 1:29b):

"...Behold, the Lamb of God, which taketh away the sin of the World."

Beloved, if the whole world is loved by God, and if Jesus came to take away the sins of the world, then there is hope for the whole world to be saved. Primarily, we must begin to see ourselves as God sees us, and speak as He speaks concerning the salvation of the world. The city of Nineveh is a good example. It took only one of God's servants, on a single occasion, to bring Nineveh to repentance. If it were possible for Nineveh, one of Israel's arch enemies, then I believe Christ's atonement has definitely brought hope to us. I pray for the fear of the Lord to overtake all who hear the Gospel message in Africa, Asia, North America, South America, Australia, and Europe; for this is the beginning of wisdom. Nineveh's account is written in Jonah 3:1, 2, and 10:

"And the word of the LORD came unto Jonah the second time, saying, Arise, go unto Nineveh, that great city, and preach unto it the preaching that I bid thee. And God saw their works, that they turned from their evil way; and God repented of the evil, that He had said that He would do unto them; and he did it not."

Let us learn some general but valuable lessons here:

1. Jonah did not take a unilateral decision to go, but was commanded by the LORD. It is one thing to be sent by the LORD and another thing to send yourself.
2. Those who are sent by others or by themselves don't usually succeed or prosper in accordance with God's standards and purpose.

3. When one is commissioned by the Lord, he/she dares not be afraid of any obstacle or opposition (spiritual or physical). The LORD of Hosts always cares for and protects His servants.

4. When sent by the Lord, one's power to accomplish the task is inherent or resident in his/her commission.

5. Everyone sent by the Lord will prevail and persevere despite the many challenges and trials. He/she will emerge, bringing in many sheaves along the way.

6. God holds accountable those who have been sent; He counts on their commitment and faithfulness.

   Beloved, have you been sent? Do you know who sent you?

   Lessons to be learned from the Ninevians:

   a. After hearing God's Word, the Ninevians believed the LORD and His prophet (Jonah 3:5).

   b. God will save whom He has destined to be saved; He will save even the vilest sinner because He is sovereign. God is reaching out to you, but you must first believe in Him. Until you trust in the Lord with all your heart, you cannot have a relationship with Him.

   c. The leadership in Nineveh believed God. They acted upon their faith with certain degree of urgency by taking the following actions:

      i. For the fear of God and for the love of their own people, they proclaimed a three-day fast. Neither food nor water was taken by both men and beasts.

      ii. The fast was led by the leadership. This is the key reason for the cooperation of the entire populace. They followed their leader's exemplary act of obedience without reservations.

A true Christian leader is known by his sincere love for God, which naturally extends to God's people.

d. Nineveh turned away from its evil and violence. Rightly so, the people's belief was backed by their obedience and total submission. This is the kind of repentance that provokes the heart of God to release blessings in abundance.

e. If you desire to see the full measure of God at work in your life, then you must be determined to get rid of evil.

f. There is no cry for a nation that moves God more than the cry that comes from the heart of a repentant people. In the case of Nineveh, the leadership assumed responsibility and took the initiative that led to their transformation.

If America and the rest of the world should be saved, the Body of Christ must rise to the occasion. Believers are the only catalysts for godly change on the earth. Haven't we already received our authority from the Lord? Yes, we have! Hasn't the Lord promised to answer when we call? Indeed, He has! Listen to what II Chronicles 7:14 assures us: ***"If my people, which are called by my name, shall humble themselves, and pray, and seek my face, and turn from their wicked ways; then will I hear from heaven, and will forgive their sin, and will heal their land."***

C. Again, Who Can be Saved? "The Whosoever"

In the Gospel of John 3:16, the Word of the Lord says,

> ***"For God so loved the world that He gave His only begotten Son, that WHOSOEVER believeth on Him should not perish, but have everlasting life."***

The salvation that God has provided is not just for a particular group of people. More so, it is for the "***whosoever.***" This refers to anyone. It could be the Mary Magdalenes, murderers, prostitutes, drug addicts, abusers, molesters, or the worst of all sinners, as Paul declared himself to be. We know the Lord saved and raised him up to be a mighty apostle for His kingdom, called specifically to the Gentile world.

In addition, the *"whosoever"* could be the poorest person from *"West Point"* (an impoverished community in my homeland, considered to be one of the worst *slums*). In contrast, the *"whosoever"* could also be the aristocrats in their mansions or the kings in their palaces, or business men, bankers or wall street experts. Anyone bearing the burden of sin can be the *"whosoever."* Again, who then can be saved?

D. The Foreknown, the Predestinate, and the Called (Romans 8:29, 31)

1. 1.   The Foreknown: The word foreknowledge is that aspect of God's supernatural wisdom and knowledge (His Omniscience) that relates to the future. This is God's ability to accurately predict the most minute and/or detailed outlook into the future of all His creation: from the inception of one's life to the end. That is to say, your successes, failures, trials, victories, joys, sorrows and where your soul will spend eternity – nothing is or will ever be hidden from Him. In His foreknowledge, God even knows who will be saved and who will not. Therefore, in the fullness of time, God will certainly save all whom He has destined to save.

2. The Predestinate: Here, God purposes in grace to bring to pass that which He foreknew, proposed, and elected. This could include one's calling or charge by God to a particular ministry or function which was foreknown before the foundations of the world. If you have been predestinated, God will save you at all costs.

3. The Called/Elect: They are the foreknown and the predestinated of the LORD God; those He foreknew would accept Him. They are those for whom He has a particular destination. Because God possesses the

wisdom and ability to know beforehand all those who will yield to His salvation call, He has already written the names of the called/elect in His Book of Life.

Let's use the man Moses as an example. God knew Moses before he was born, and destined him to deliver Israel from the bondage of the Egyptians. In God's providence, He protected and guided Moses from birth until the fullness of his ministry. In the appointed season, God literally appeared to Moses and commissioned him for the redemption of Israel. In Jeremiah 1:4, 5, we have an example of the foreknowledge, the predestination, and the call of God on the life of the Prophet Jeremiah:

"Then the word of the LORD came unto me, saying, Before I formed thee in the belly I knew thee; and before thou camest forth out of the womb I sanctified thee, and I ordained thee a prophet unto the nations."

And Romans 8:29, 30 confirm every Word in Jeremiah's life

"For whom He did foreknow, He also did predestinate to be conformed to the image of His Son, that he might be the firstborn among many brethren. Moreover whom He did predestinate, them He also called: and whom He called, them He also justified: and whom He justified, them He also glorified."

My friend, are you one of the elects or called out ones? If yes, then I bless God for you. The fact that you have accepted Jesus Christ as your Savior and Lord, makes you one of His chosen. If you have not made this decision by now, you are still lost. I want to assure you that Christ loves you, nonetheless. As far as God is concerned, His perfect will for you is to be saved. To make this a reality, your human will is called into play. This means that you must allow your flesh to give way to God's Spirit; your imperfect will must bow to the perfect and glorious will of the Lord.

E. The Lost Can be Saved

In Luke 19:10, the Lord Jesus said these powerful Words:

"For the Son of man is come to seek and to save that which was lost." The Lord Jesus truly came to save the lost souls of the world. They live outside of Christ, and seek the things of the flesh and not the things of the Spirit. Remember that God loves you. His love seeks and delivers you, whoever and wherever you may be. Once more who can be saved?

F. A Household Can be Saved

In Acts 16:31, Paul and Silas by the Spirit, answered the jailer and said: *"... Believe on the Lord Jesus Christ, and thou shalt be saved; and thy house."*

When salvation enters a home, it is not only meant for that individual member of the family, but also for the entire family. In the case of my family, I became the first to receive Christ only through the grace of the Lord. Over a period of time, the "salvation fever" was transmitted to my siblings, and later to my father, who gave his life to Christ during my marriage ceremony. Then after several years my mother also received Christ.

Likewise, when the Lord Jesus entered Cornelius' house, his entire family received salvation. They were then baptized with the Holy Ghost and with fire:

"While Peter yet spake these words, the Holy Spirit fell on all them which heard the word. And they of the circumcision which

believed were astonished, as many as came with Peter, because that on the Gentiles also was poured out the gift of the Holy Spirit. For they heard them speak with tongues, and magnify God..." (Acts 10:44-46).

Indeed, all of these true life-changing events are wonderful examples of Christ's great love and desire to save you and your household. I hope they will encourage you.

God's promises are true. Take Him at His Word and believe that He is able to transform your life and even use you to change what may seem to be impossible situations or circumstances in the lives of your spouse, your children, as well as your extended family.

[Prayer]: I command every devil hindering your household from being saved, to bow and be crushed at God's Word, in Jesus' mighty name. Amen. For this year shall not pass until you have seen God's Word being fulfilled in the life of your family members, in Jesus' powerful name, Amen! In the mighty name of Jesus Christ of Nazareth, I break every stronghold that has hindered the salvation of your family, Amen.

G. Again, Who can be Saved? All Sinners Can be Saved

Is it really possible for all sinners to be saved? Yes! There is one obvious condition – only if they believe in the redemptive work of Christ – or be lost forever. We remember the words of Paul in Romans 3:23. *"For all have sinned, and come short of the glory of God."*

I cannot overly stress how essential it is for us all to truly bear in mind that in the eyes of God, no sinner is beyond His reach, no matter how vicious or treacherous his/her life can be. Christ's precious blood is able to cleanse every sin and heal the sin-sick heart. As vile a sinner as Paul was, God in his mercy saved him (I Timothy 1:15):

"This is a faithful saying, and worthy of all acceptation, that Christ Jesus came into the world to save sinners; of whom I am chief."

Let us also take a peek into the life of Manasseh; he was one of the kings of the Northern kingdom of Israel. Manasseh ruled longer than all the kings of both the Northern and Southern kingdoms, but was extremely wicked. Here are some highlights of his reign (II Kings 21: 2):

"And he did that which was evil in the sight of the LORD, after the abominations of the heathen, whom the LORD cast out before the children of Israel."

Despite all, Manasseh experienced God's forgiveness when he repented and turned to Him (II Chronicles 33:11-13):

"Wherefore the LORD brought upon them the captains of the host of the king of Assyria, which took Manasseh among the thorns, and bound him with fetters, and carried him to Babylon. And when he was in affliction, he besought the LORD his God, and humbled himself greatly before the God of his fathers, and prayed unto Him: and He was entreated of him, and heard his supplication, and brought him again to Jerusalem into his kingdom. Then Manasseh knew that the LORD He was God."

As stated in these verses, Manasseh remained in his state of wickedness, and did not repent of his sins until he was afflicted by the King of Babylon. We observe that Manasseh would not have received God's judgment if, in the first place, he had embraced the love of God that was in easy reach. This is a lesson for everyone: that pride is rebellion, and rebellion is disobedience or sin. The Scriptures say pride cometh before a fall, but a broken and contrite heart is humility before God. A person with such a subdued virtue, He has promised to honor.

We must be grateful to God for sending His own Son in the Person of JESUS CHRIST THE RIGHTEOUS, who became afflicted and wounded for our sins. This is a high honor exhibited on our behalf. In II Corinthians 5:21 we read these Words: ***"For He made Him to be sin for us, who knew no sin; that we might be made the righteousness of God in Him."***

Beloved, Jesus our Lord literally took the place of every sinner on the cross. This is why every sinner can be saved if he/she believes on Him.

Again, who can be saved?

H. The Many Can be Saved

How many people can be saved, someone may ask. As many as believe and receive Jesus Christ as their Savior and Lord. The writer of the book of St. John testifies of this by the Spirit of the living God: ***"But as many as received him, to them gave he power to become the sons of God; even to them that believe on his name"*** (John1:12).

How many does God want to be saved among the Gentiles? As many as will believe and confess Jesus as Lord and Savior. We learn from Scriptures that the Gentiles were those born outside the Jewish race, those for whom salvation was not meant. But thanks be to God, the grace of the Messiah has delivered us from darkness and brought us into His marvelous light. That same grace unlimited, full, and free is not just for a few, but is now available to save ***MANY*** lives. I mean, ***ALL OF HUMANITY*** that would believe on His name. And so, the limitation to salvation is not from God's perspective. It is especially blamed on those to whom the offer has been made to receive His FREE GIFT, but they continue to reject it. Only those who accept this offer will, of course, benefit therefrom. In John 1:11, 12, the Word of God reveals that: "He came unto His own, and His own received Him not. But as many as received Him, to them gave He power to become the sons of God, even to them that believe on His name." It is in this light that only the many who receive this gift of salvation can be saved. My last word to you in response to the question, who can be saved, is as follows:

I. He Who 'Believes' Can be Saved

When the Master gave His disciples the Great Commission to present the Gospel message to the world, He said those who would be saved are the ones who would believe His Word. Read St. Mark 16:15, 16:

> *"And He said unto them, Go ye into all the world, and preach the gospel to every creature. He that believeth and is baptized shall be saved; but he that believeth not shall be damned."*

Let us scrutinize the word "baptize." Is baptism a qualification for salvation? My answer is No! Baptism in itself has no power to save. Although the Lord commanded it in His Great Commission, salvation is purely the saving of one's spirit, soul and body.

There are many who hold the view that unless you are baptized, your salvation is incomplete. However, the Biblical view is that if you are not saved or born again, baptism has no value; it has no impact on you. But after you have become a child of God, do everything possible to get baptized. You must understand that baptism is only a symbol of identification with Christ's birth, death and resurrection:

1. You have died with Him by putting to death your old sinful ways, and you are henceforth no longer your own, but you belong to the Lord Jesus.

2. You and your old lifestyle have been symbolically buried with Christ by your emersion under water.
3. You have been risen with Christ by your rise out of the water. You are now a new person in Christ, ready to serve Him in Spirit and in truth.

The choice is yours, whether to accept Jesus Christ as Savior and live in eternal bliss; or reject Him and suffer the consequences of everlasting damnation, deprivation and death, separated from God's holy and eternal presence. There is no escape for those who abandon the Lord. I urge you to choose Jesus today and be blessed now and forever. In John 5:24, we have this glorious promise from the mouth of Jesus Christ Himself:

> *"Verily, verily, I say unto you, He that heareth my word, and believeth on Him that sent me, hath everlasting life, and shall not come into condemnation; but is passed from death unto life."*

CHAPTER FIVE

THE GLORIOUS WORK OF THE TRIUNE GOD IN BRINGING REDEMPTION/ SALVATION TO MANKIND

A. God the Father – His Work in the Plan of Redemption

1. **God Designed the Plan and Ordained it Before the Foundations of the World**

In God's foreknowledge concerning the future events of the world, He knew that Adam was capable of sinning and would eventually fall. As such, the Lord God preplanned Adam's salvation, as well as the salvation of all mankind. He achieved this in the First Adam long before the world was formed. In this respect, Adam's failure was not a shock to the LORD.

a. In His divine plan, we have already learned that God knew all who would be saved, from eternity past to future eternity: ***"For whom He did foreknow, He also did predestinate to be conformed to the image of His Son, that he might be the firstborn among many brethren"***

(Romans. 8:29). The important point I want to inject here is that, even though God has foreknowledge of those who would refuse His salvation offer, in no way is He responsible for the sins and defiance of men. Adam had the freedom of choice; so do you!

What, then, are the responsibilities of believers, with regard to fostering God's salvation plan, so that we can influence people in making right choices? Believers' obligations extend beyond guaranteeing their own salvation. Once we have come to know the Lord, He intends to use us as His **hands and feet** to spread the Good News to others and disciple them in the faith. And the one that is preached to must exercise his/her God given choice to accept His free gift of salvation. Our obedience is then blessed by the Lord, there is a rippled effect, and untold numbers of lost people become saved.

b. In His divine plan, God chose you and me to be conformed into the image of Christ before we came into this world. God Himself voted for us to be a part of His divine plan of salvation. For anything to manifest in this realm of the physical world, it first has to be made and ordained in the spirit world. Since it is the spirit world that created the physical world, God guaranteed that you and I were saved and ordained for His purpose on the earth before He ordered our physical birth (Jeremiah 1:5).

c. God in His divine plan called you and me in the realm of the spirit and manifested the call in the earthly realm. *"Moreover whom He predestinate, them He also called: and whom He called, them He also justified: and whom He justified, them He also glorified"* *(Roman 8:30).* Therefore, my call into God's plan of redemption and ordination to His ministry was predetermined in the Spirit before it actually took place in November 1973 on a Sunday evening between 6-7 p.m. In other words, I was called by the Lord before the actual physical manifestation took place in Monrovia, Liberia, West Africa and the rest of the world. I count this as a great privilege to be called and chosen by the Lord to fulfill my part in the execution of His plan and purpose for my life. I thank God that because He is a God of perfection, He makes no mistakes.

As a minister of the Lord Jesus Christ, I urge you to remain in your calling and be faithful and diligent. Remember the call of God is the highest calling in the whole wide world. Beloved, please take God's call upon your life very seriously.

2. **God spoke the plan prophetically in the Garden of Eden:** *"and I will put enmity between thee and the woman, and between thy seed and her seed; it shall bruise thy head, and thou shalt bruise his heel" (Genesis 3:15).*

When God released those Words, salvation was as good as done. For when God speaks, in His mind, it has already taken place.

By God's declaration, the redemption of man was put in place, ready to be executed at the appointed time. By His affirmation, the power of the enemy was broken from over all mankind, especially those who would receive His Son's salvation. By divine proclamation, you and I were created and became a part of God's redemptive plan. This has rendered our common enemy, Satan, impotent.

3. **God Executed His Plan of Salvation in the Fullness of Time**

   a. By sending His Son of Love (Galatians 4: 4, 5): *"But when the fullness of the time was come, God sent forth His Son, made of a woman, made under the law, To redeem them that were under the law, that we might receive the adoption of sons".*

The sending of Jesus by the Father is a clear manifestation of God's unending love for mankind. There is no sin problem you have that Jesus cannot handle. He is God's perfect solution for you. Jesus is the first and last answer that the Father has released. So blessed are you if you believe God's report.

b. By giving His Son to be the sacrifice on every man's behalf. This is seen in John 3:16, and II Corinthians 5: 21: *"For God so loved the world, that He gave His only begotten Son, that whosoever believeth in Him should not perish, but have everlasting life" (John 3:16).*

"For He hath made Him to be sin for us, who knew no sin; that we might be made the righteousness of God in Him" (II Corinthians 5:21).

God views Christ as the best, the One and only sacrifice, whose death was efficacious to take away your guilt and bondages. His blood is the purest liquid that washes away sins.

c. By drawing people unto Jesus for salvation: *"No man can come to Me, except the Father which hath sent Me draw him: and I will raise him up at the last day" (John 6:44).*

Beloved, Christ's sacrifice had to be accomplished for your total redemption. His divine energy is set in order for your freedom. You don't have to go to Jerusalem or Mecca, neither do you have to join or go to a Church to be saved. Even though attending Church is necessary to hear the Gospel preached, to foster growth, to fellowship and to worship the Lord, it is not a prerequisite to salvation.

If you are not saved, you can receive Christ right now, wherever you are! In Revelation 3:20 the Lord Jesus said, *"Behold, I stand at the door, and knock: if any man hear my voice, and open the door, I will come in to him, and will sup with him, and he with Me."* Are you ready and willing to make this important decision at once? Until you are saved by the blood of Jesus, you are exposed to the snares of the devil. [Prayer]: *I prophesy your salvation today, in Jesus' name!*

B. God the Son – His Work in the Plan of Salvation.

1. Jesus became like us in order to save us (Philippians 2: 5, 11):

    "Let this mind be in you, which was also in Christ Jesus: Who, being in the form of God, thought it not robbery to be equal with God: But made Himself of no reputation, and took upon Him the form of a servant, and was made in the likeness of men: And being found in fashion as a man, He humbled Himself, and became obedient unto death, even the death of the cross."

Have you ever wondered why God didn't send an angel to redeem mankind, instead of sacrificing the life of His precious Son? The study of the Scriptures present several factual basis:

a. Angels are spirit beings that are holy.
b. Angels do not have flesh and blood; they have had glorified bodies since their creation.
c. Angels do not physically grow or mature in any form; they were created perfect.
d. Angels were not the best God had for the sacrificial offering of our sins. Christ was.

Christ Jesus was the only PERFECT AND GLORIOUS sacrifice made possible to save man and satisfy the holy justice of God through

His shed blood and atonement. Praise His Holy name! Apostle Laurore declared this: ***"The value of the sacrifice determines the quality of the life of the person."*** Jesus' death for you and me meant something important to the LORD. Thus, we should never take for granted what Christ has done for us on the cross. Here are some specific reasons why we ought to take Christ's death very seriously:

2. Jesus Died for us That We Might Live unto God

a. Jesus died to destroy Satan, who had the power of death (Hebrews 2:14)

> ***"Forasmuch then as the children are partakers of flesh and blood, He also Himself likewise took part of the same; that through death he might destroy him that had the power of death, that is, the devil;"***

Satan had four powers before the coming of our Lord Jesus Christ:

i   The power of sin – if you know your authority in Christ as a believer, no more does sin have dominion over you. You now have authority over sin. In Christ, you are able to say no to drugs, smoking, pre-marital and extra-marital sex, alcohol, as well as all other sins.

ii The power of sickness – as a believer, you are no longer under the control of the demons of diseases or sicknesses.

iii The power of poverty – poverty has no more bearing on your life as a child of God.

iv The power of death – in Christ, we are passed from death to life.

Jesus, therefore, dismantled every barrier and repossessed these powers from Satan, so as to reestablish our dominion on the earth.

b. Jesus died to destroy the works of the devil (I John 3: 8b):

"...For this purpose the Son of God was manifested, that he might destroy the works of the devil."

When Jesus raised Lazarus from the dead, He was destroying the works of the devil. In Mark 5:1-13, when the Master cast out all those demons from the life of the Gadarene, He was also destroying the works of the devil.

When Jesus rescued me, Anthony F. B. Tarnue from the bloody hands of Satan in the secret society or bush school, He was destroying the works of the devil against my life. The act of salvation in the lives of people today means, God is setting sinners free from demonism, drugs, alcoholism, corruption, depression, witchcraft, and many immoral acts including sexual perversions: homosexuality, lesbianism, transgenderism, rape and sexual abuse. The Almighty is definitely destroying the works of the devil!

[Prayer]: *Now, I pray that you will experience God's delivering power in your life right now, in Jesus' name, Amen. I command every devil that has been operating in your life to flee from you now, in Jesus' name, Amen. Be loosed from any entanglement of Satan, in Jesus' name, Amen.*

Beloved, if you have been searching for freedom from every harassment and embarrassment of the devil, today is that day. [Prayer]: *Be freed from your infirmities, in Jesus' name. I pray for God's power to come upon you now, in Jesus' name, Amen.* If you believe in this prayer, you will never be the same again.

c. Jesus died to remove every demonic handwriting of ordinance and evil pronouncement against us: ***"Blotting out the handwriting of ordinances that was against us, which was contrary to us, and took it out of*** *the way, nailing it to his cross;" (Colossians 2:14).* These ordinances comprise, but are not limited to, certain ungodly acts or practices in our culture; every negative word pronounced upon you prior to or after your physical birth, and every evil covenant that may have been made on your behalf. All of these have been destroyed today, by the precious blood of Jesus.

d. Jesus died and rose again to disarm and disgrace Satan and his cohorts on our behalf (2:15): *"And having spoiled principalities and powers, He made a shew of them openly, triumphing over them in it."* As we heartily cling to this knowledge and belief, we as believers can confidently proclaim that since Christ, the Head, has triumphed over Satan, we too have the victory. Satan and all his demons in every home, in every village, in every town, in every city, in every state and in every nation and kingdom have all been put under our feet.

With Jesus' disarmament of the enemy, we have the assurance and power to fearlessly rise up and declare that his power of sin, fear, sicknesses, diseases, adversities and death, no more have any rule over the saints of God. Remember the Words of the Lord in Luke 10:19: *"Behold, I give unto you power to tread on serpents and scorpions, and over all the power of the enemy: and nothing shall by any means hurt you."* Here are my petitions unto the Father for you:

[Prayer 1]: *"Be freed from every fear of the devil, in Jesus' name, Amen.*

[Prayer 2]: *"I pray from today, as you have surrendered your life to Jesus, sin, sickness, fear, death, and poverty will have no more power over you, in Jesus' mighty name, Amen.*

[Prayer] 3: *"Be freed from yourself, in Jesus' name, Amen.*

[Prayer] 4: *"You will fulfill God's plan for your life, in Jesus' name, Amen.*

[Prayer] 5: *"I pray that with the pregnancy of Jesus in your belly, you will deliver on time, in Jesus' name, Amen.*

3. Jesus Became our Substitute on the Cross: ***"For Christ also hath once suffered for sins, the just for the unjust, that he might bring us to God, being put to death in the flesh, but quickened by the Spirit:"*** **(I Peter 3:18).**

Dr. Willmington states that the substitutionary work of Christ has two phases:

a. Temporary substitution– during the Old Testament period before Calvary, temporary substitution meant that the sheep would die for the shepherd (Genesis 22:10-13).

*"**And Abraham lifted up his eyes, and looked, and behold behind him a ram caught in a thicket by his horns: and Abraham went and took the ram, and offered him up for a burnt offering in the stead of his son"** (Genesis 22:13).*

Substitution, whether spiritual or physical, means the act of replacing someone or something with another person or thing. The Old Testament sacrifices were temporary for various reasons:

    i.   The sacrifices were not perfect.
    ii. They had no power to take away sin.
    iii. They brought no change to the individuals for whom the sacrifices were made.
    iv. They limited individuals from true fellowship with the Lord.

b. One lamb for one family (Exodus 12: 3, 4):

> *"Speak ye unto all the congregation of Israel, saying, In the tenth day of this month they shall take to them every man a lamb, according to the house of their fathers, a lamb for an house: And if the household be too little for the lamb, let him and his neighbor next unto his house take it according to the number of the souls; every man according to his eating shall make your count for the lamb."*

This sacrifice was a lamb offering for one family. That is, one lamb to a single household. If a household were too little, then they were to allow their immediate next door neighbor to join with them, according to the number of persons in that family.

c. Permanent substitution – This was a one-time only sacrifice, the best and easiest of all sacrifices.

The substitutionary work of Christ in the New Testament relates to the death of the shepherd for the sheep: our Lord Jesus was that shepherd. Look at John 10:11: *"I am the good shepherd: the good shepherd giveth his life for the sheep."*

Jesus became sin for us that we might become the righteousness of God in Christ Jesus (II Corinthians 5: 21). Someone once said, (which I believe is a true statement about Jesus Christ): **"The Son of God became the Son of Man that sons of men might become sons of God."**

4. **Jesus Became our Propitiation unto God**

> *"And He is the propitiation for our sins: and not for ours only, but also for the sins of the whole world" (I John 2:2).*

What is propitiation? It means to render favor, to satisfy a just demand, to appease a righteous and an angry heart from sin. When Jesus' blood was drawn from the cross and poured upon the mercy seat of heaven, it pacified God's wrath and judgment against sin in our lives. This means that God can now look at what Christ has done on our behalf and smile at us. Praise Jesus!

5. **Jesus Became our Reconciliation**

According to Evans, reconciliation is the act of Christ whereby His shed blood on the cross removed the enmity between God and man, placing man back in fellowship with God (Ephesians 2:16; Colossians 1:20-22; Romans 5:10; Matthew 5:24).

Willmington explains it in this way:

a. That there are two implications of reconciliation:
    1. A previous animosity existed and
    2. The offended party now views things differently.

b. There are two phases of reconciliation:
    1. God was in Christ reconciling the world unto Himself. God did this when He Himself bore our sins on the cross through His Son Jesus Christ, giving us peace and rest:

    "And all things are of God, who hath reconciled us to Himself by Jesus Christ, and hath given to us the ministry of reconciliation; to wit that God was in Christ, reconciling the world unto himself, not imputing their trespasses unto them; and hath committed unto us the word of reconciliation" (II Corinthians 5:18, 19).

2. Man now has the responsibility to reconcile himself to God through Christ:

    a. Through the preaching of the Gospel of Christ. This mandate given to every believer, is to broadcast the Gospel.

    b. By your fervent prayers for lost souls.

    c. By your strong financial support.

    d. By consecrating and committing your own personal life to the cause of Christ. That is, live in the way that attracts sinners to Christ. Be a shining light to the world.

"Now then we are ambassadors for Christ, as though God did beseech you by us: We pray you in Christ's stead, be ye reconciled to God" (5:20).

c. This is the chronological order of reconciliation:

    1. In the Garden, God and man faced each other in glorious fellowship. They were once **friends.**

    2. After the fall, God and man turned away from each other and they became enemies.

    3. At Calvary, ***God turned His face back towards man. They became reconciled.***

    4. Then at conversion, by the confession of Jesus as his Lord and Savior, ***man now turns his face towards God.***

6. **Jesus was cursed for You and Me:**

"Christ hath redeemed us from the curse of the law, being made a curse for us: for it is written, CURSED IS EVERY ONE THAT HANGETH ON A TREE: that the blessing of Abraham might

come on the Gentiles through Jesus Christ; that we might receive the promise of the Spirit through faith" (Galatians 3:13, 14).

What was the curse of the Law? The concept of the curse of the Law comes from the premise that unbelievers or those living outside of God's blessings are under divine condemnation due to sin. This is especially serious in situations where people defiantly oppose or actively reject the Word and Work of God (Galatians 1:8, 9; II Peter 2:14; Revelation 16:9, 11, 21).

Throughout this book, I have attempted to present the many curses of the Law, among which are the three major categories of deaths (spiritual, physical and the second death). In passing, I urge you to remember that believers are totally released from any appearance of death due to the assurance of the free gift of salvation: Our new birth has given us total redemption and renewal of our spirits, souls and bodies. We have regained our authority and power over the earth from Satan (Luke 10:19). The abundance of God's presence in our lives gives us spiritual richness and when we finally depart this world, we sleep in perfect peace and rest with hope in our resurrected and glorified Lord. He has promised to be right there to joyfully welcome us into eternity with Him forever. What a wonderful, and blessed reward (I Thessalonians 4:13-18).

It is my sincere prayer that the Lord will reveal His truth to all disobedient people who may be privileged to hear His call to salvation. Indeed, procrastination is a deadly weapon and dangerous trick of the enemy. Take action now and save yourself from eternal doom! When you are saved, salvation will also come to your household at the appointed time (Acts 16:25-31).

Does this refer to you? If yes, I am sure the effects of your sins are apparent, because sin is nothing but sin! Do you desire godly prosperity, so that once and for all, you and your family can escape spiritual bankruptcy at all levels of your lives? Do you want your children to avoid self-destruction and desist from causing you unnecessary problems? If you want to escape these insanities of Satan, then take the lead in turning to God today:

"For ye know the grace of our Lord Jesus Christ, that, though He was rich, yet for your sakes He became poor, that ye through His poverty might be rich" (II Corinthians 8:9).

It is crucial that one thinks before acting and listens and reasons before making decisions in life. You must know that your life is wrapped up and woven in God's plan, not yours (Galatians 6:7; Jeremiah 29:11). Throughout your life, you must trust God totally and rely on His wisdom and direction (Proverbs 3:5, 6). This is about righteousness and unrighteousness; faith, as opposed to faithlessness; rest, instead of anxiety; peace versus distress; joy, not sorrow.

[**Prayer**]: *Receive the grace to make right choices in life, in Jesus' name. From this day forward, every choice you make will add color to your life. In Jesus' precious name you will not suffer again!*

Please regard highly these admonitions and Biblical illustrations to prevent unnecessary pain and sufferings in your life:

1. You ***Must*** avoid, suppress, turn away from, and eliminate ***PERSONAL SIN.*** They could lead to sicknesses and diseases in your life. Take a look at John 5:14:

    "Afterward Jesus findeth him in the temple, and said unto him, Behold, thou art made whole: sin no more, lest a worse thing come unto thee" (v. 14).

a. Use your **TONGUE WISELY.** Let your words build others up and encourage them, instead of tearing them apart (Numbers 12:1-10).

> *"And Miriam and Aaron spake against Moses because of the Ethiopian woman whom he had married: for he had married an Ethiopian woman. And they said, hath the LORD indeed spoken only by Moses? Hath he not spoken also by us? And the LORD heard it" (v.v. 1 & 2).*

The apostle James cautions believers to bridle their tongues. The analogy of bridling the tongue relates to what happens to a horse whose mouth is buckled with bits and reins to allow for proper control. Christ is the Master of our lives. As our guardian, His Holy Spirit wants to be able to control our tongues if we allow Him.

When we turn our hearts over to Christ, His love exploding in us compels us to please Him and to treat others with love, compassion and respect. The love we give to others should reflect the love we continue to receive from our Savior. An uncontrollable tongue does serve as a poison to the victim and eventually to the perpetrator.

b. ***Do not CASTIGATE GOD'S ANOINTED:*** I want you to take a good look at the caliber of ministers that received God's judgment. Aaron was anointed by the LORD as the High Priest for all of Israel; Miriam was a mighty prophetess, a glorious singer, surrogate mother and sister of Moses.

When Aaron and Miriam used their tongues against God's anointed representative, their sin grieved the heart of the LORD, and they were duly punished. To speak against God's chosen leader is expressed rebellion against God Himself. God is unchangeable and He judges without discrimination. While He loves sinners, He hates sin, cannot tolerate it, and has declared that no sin will ever go unpunished. Believers are called to pray relentlessly for their leaders.

2. Be Aware of Generational Sins

Generational sins are those that are passed unto succeeding generations as consequences for the sins, iniquities or transgressions of past generations that are related biologically to them. They may also be defined as curses placed upon one's life due to the satanic covenant(s) entered into by an individual's past generation(s):

> *"And God spake all these words, saying, I am the LORD thy God, which have brought thee out of the land of Egypt, out of the house of bondage. Thou shalt have no other gods before me; Thou shalt not make unto thee any graven image, or any likeness of anything that is in heaven above, or that is in the earth beneath, or that is in the water under the earth: Thou shalt not bow down thyself to them, nor serve them: for I the LORD thy God am a jealous God, visiting the iniquity of the fathers upon the children unto the third and fourth generation of them that hate me;" (Exodus 20:1-5).*

If iniquity is not rejected and denounced, and if such curses are not broken, one may continue to suffer from the dreadful attacks of the enemy in the form of curses such as: murder, sexual and other kinds of immoralities, drug/alcohol abuse, various blood covenants, involvement with the occult, witchcraft or voodoo practices, enchantments or satanic worship, "meditations" and even unpaid and unfulfilled promises or vows. Below are some examples of satanic activities in which my family and tribe were involved:

a. Worship of the ancestors' spirits or animism – the spirits of the ancestors were appeased for good luck, or to provoke their blessings.

b. Direct contact with Satan in the secret *(poro/sande)* societies or bush schools.

c. Initiation – this called for the extraction of an appreciable amount of blood. It was a major requirement to seal the people's covenant with the demons.

d. Contact with familiar spirits – this comprised communicating with the dead in the spirit world.

e. Village covenant – at times, human sacrifices were made to supposedly "keep the village safe."

f. Witchcraft – high class rituals in which the members transformed themselves at night from humans into witches.

In addition to the above, several other covenants with Satan are responsible for many sicknesses, diseases, poverty or deaths. While these demonic occurrences may vary from place to place, they are the same tactical operations of the devil (Satan).

It's very important for you to understand that these curses will manifest in the form of suppressive control and exploitation of one's life by an unseen enemy – all the more reason why it is crucial for everyone to be covered under the blood of Jesus.

Friend, please keep reading until you come to the end where I have laid out prayers for your deliverance.

3. Be Aware of National Sins

Curses that come upon a nation because of the wickedness of its leader(s), past or present, are called national sins. These curses are usually demonstrated through the breaking of God's laws; any involvement with the devil, namely: idolatry; broken covenant(s) with the Lord; racism; discrimination and corruption, coupled with all other types of social, economic, and political injustices.

During the days of David, a curse came upon the entire nation of Israel because of the sins of its leaders. It happened that the Gibeonites, one of Israel's enemies, had heard of the manifestation of God's power in Israel, giving them victory in every battle over their enemies. Under pretense and hypocrisy, the Gibeonites succeeded in tricking Joshua and the princes of Israel to believe they were not enemies, but ambassadors traveling from afar to make peace. Little did Joshua realize the Gibeonites were actually their neighbors; inhabitants of the same nation God had previously commanded him to destroy. And so, under the leadership of Joshua, the Israelites unilaterally entered into a peace covenant with their enemies without regard for the LORD. The Gibeonites were permitted to reside among them and be protected by their army. Thus, under this league, Israel couldn't destroy their own enemies as God had commanded. Surely, this was an act of disobedience and an offense against the LORD. As a consequence, the LORD did not reveal to them the true identity and ulterior motive of the Gibeonites (Joshua 9:14-21).

It was not until many years later, during the reign of King David, successor to King Saul, that the curse upon Israel actually took effect. In that account, we observe that King Saul had personally decided to break the ***vow*** Joshua had made with the Gibeonites by slaying them. No doubt, the consequence of Saul's outrageous offense led to the national curse. The Bible says, "It was meant for Saul and his bloody house because he killed the Gibeonites." This is a clear example of the high essence the LORD places on His children to honor every vow or covenant made before Him (II Samuel 21:1 and Ecclesiastes 5:4-6).

"Then there was a famine in the days of David three years, year after year; and David enquired of the LORD. And the LORD

79

answered, It is for Saul, and for his bloody house, because he slew the Gibeonites" (II Samuel 21:1).

Even though Saul was dead, the past sins of the former leader of Israel came upon the whole nation. When David inquired of the LORD, He responded by saying, "A curse was already on the nation…" The only recourse to the removal of the curse against Israel was for a restitution to be made against the house of Saul – and his seven sons were hanged:

"Righteousness exalteth a nation: but sin is a reproach to any people" (Proverb 14:34).

4. Pray for the **REVELATION** of the Lord

The lack of revelation is the sorrowful plight of many people today. It has left them vulnerable to the enemy, thus leading them astray. I pray that you will open up your heart to receive this manifestation and become a partaker of the *"blessing"* of Abraham. For Christ, who became a curse for us all, has redeemed us with His own blood from every curse of the Law.

C. God the Holy Spirit – His Work of Redemption: His Ministry in God's Plan of Salvation for all People

1. His ministry concerning the Lord Jesus Christ, the Savior

a. Jesus our Savior was begotten by the Holy Spirit (Luke 1:35):

"And the angel answered and said unto her, The Holy Ghost shall come upon thee, and the power of the Highest shall overshadow thee: therefore also that holy thing which shall be born of thee shall be called the Son of God."

The immaculate conception of the virgin Mary could have been nothing other than the supernatural act of a powerful, sovereign and loving God (Luke 1:34,35). While some religions of the world question the validity of God having a wife, much more a son, we Christians believe that every Word of God is true and the truth lies in His Word.

The character of the Most High speaks of His holiness, which is the complete perfection of His other attributes. It is by expressing faith in Christ that we are saved, and it is by the same faith that His Word is accepted and established in our hearts.

b. Jesus our Savior was anointed by the Holy Spirit (Luke 4:18,19).

c. Jesus our Savior was given the Holy Spirit without measure (John 3:34):

"For He whom God hath sent speaketh the words of God: for God giveth not the Spirit by measure unto Him."

Christ's possession of the Spirit without measure is an indication that:

1. The Lord Jesus was the only person who operated in all the nine gifts of the Holy Spirit. With this level of anointing, He was able to work wonders in solving every problem, whether spiritual or physical: He transformed lives; healed broken hearts; cast out demons; fed thousands; healed the sick; raised the dead and provided joy, peace and hope.

2. He operated in the fivefold ministry gifts as an apostle, a prophet, an evangelist, a pastor and a teacher (Ephesians 4:11).

3. In the demonstration of the mighty power of the Spirit, all the nine "fruit of the Spirit" bore witness in His life without limitations (Galatians 5:22, 23). He was full of love, joy and peace. He carried a great deal of longsuffering. He was all gentle and all together good. His faith always abided, He was the meekest man

on the earth in His days, and He had all levels of self-control. Praise His Holy name!

The secret to the success of the glorious ministry of the Lord Jesus Christ was completely dependent upon the fullness and the active voice of the Holy Spirit. When we allow the Holy Spirit to fill us and speak through us, our success in life and ministry becomes practically fruitful. Satan, demons, and life's problems do not obey the voices of mere men. Nonetheless, they do immediately bow to the powerful, anointed and commanding voice of the Holy Spirit.

d.   Jesus our Savior was full of the Holy Spirit (Luke 4:1):

"And Jesus being full of the Holy Ghost returned from Jordan, and was led by the Spirit into the wilderness."

e.   Jesus our Savior was led by the Holy Spirit (Matthew 4:1):

"Then was Jesus led up of the Spirit into the wilderness to be tempted of the devil."

f.   Jesus our Savior was empowered by the Holy Spirit (Matthew 12:28):

"But if I cast out devils by the Spirit of God, then the kingdom of God is come unto you."

g.   Jesus our Savior offered Himself at Calvary through the Holy Spirit (Hebrew 9:14).

h.   Jesus our Savior was raised from the dead by the Holy Spirit (Romans 1:4):

"And declared to be the Son of God with power, according to the spirit of holiness, by the resurrection from the dead:"

A story is told about a "great" man from the East who believed with all his heart that he was another savior, like Jesus. One day, a large number of people gathered together and said to him, "If you are truly a savior like Jesus as you have claimed to be, then allow us to crucify you, by hanging you on the cross where you will remain until you die. But if you are revived on the third day, then we will believe in you." The end of this matter is that, the self-proclaimed "great" man and his allegation to be another savior has since become a story.

Friend, Jesus is definitely the only Savior of the entire world. He vindicated it by His death, burial and resurrection. Jesus is alive today and forever. He can become alive in you if you are willing.

If you want to join God's winning team, it's imperative that you reject Satan, for God's winners are more than conquerors through Christ Jesus.

2. The Holy Spirit: His ministry concerning the unsaved

In John's Gospel chapter 16:7-11, the Lord gave us an outline of the precious ministry of the Holy Spirit to the unsaved:

"Nevertheless I tell you the truth; It is expedient for you that I go away: for if I go not away, the Comforter will not come unto you; but if I depart, I will send Him unto you. And when He is come, He will reprove the world of sin, and of righteousness, and of judgment: Of sin, because they believe not on Me; Of righteousness, because I go to My Father, and ye see Me no more; Of judgment, because the prince of this world is judged."

The key word in this passage is *'reprove.'* It can be classified in three categories:

i.   To convince – means the Holy Spirit will persuade sinners of their wrong doings.
ii. To convict – means to bring to light, or to convey to someone's conscience his/her evil deeds (John 8:9).
iii. Reprove carries the idea of revealing a person's fault to him/her upfront (Matthew 8:15).

We have accordingly learned that on the whole, the Holy Spirit's ministry to the unsaved is primarily aimed at:

a. Convicting them of sins (John 16:8):

"And when He is come, He will reprove the world of sin, and of righteousness, and of judgment."

As we know, sin is referring to any act of rebellion against God. Whether "great" or "small," God condemns and considers all rebellion as a direct affront and as such, sin. This may not be the popular view of the world at large, especially as it relates to unbelievers and backsliders. Some believe that murder, adultery, fornication, and perhaps idolatry or the worship of false gods are among the "greater" sins; while theft, addictions, pride, unforgiveness and lying, for example, are the "lessor" offenses, and that they don't matter.

Yes, these are all sins of commission that could be forgiven if unbelievers and those who have gone astray were to exercise their faith in the finished work of Christ and repent. However, it is the sin of rejecting Christ's atonement that would definitely lead to the spiritual death of all offenders, with eternal punishment in hell.

The emphasis here is on the question of faith or trust in the Lord, without which no man is able to please God, according to Hebrews 11:6. This is why it is so important that sinners who may fall under the conviction of the Holy Spirit respond appropriately by submitting to the Lord.

> *"But without faith it is impossible to please Him: for he that cometh to God must believe that He is, and that He is a rewarder of them that diligently seek Him" (Hebrews 11:6).*

Beloved, the Bible has no other remedy for those who refuse to believe in Jesus as the Son of God and the Savior of all mankind. Why? Because the remedy for all sin, be it small, great, personal, generational or national is the **LORD JESUS CHRIST**. He is the Lamb that died on the cross in everyone's place (John 3:16-18).

b.   He convicts man of righteousness

Righteousness means right standing with God. It carries the idea of being at peace with Him. In the below Scripture, it states firstly that the Spirit of God will point out to the unsaved that God is righteous. Secondly, that there is only one right way to get to God and that is through the Lord Jesus Christ who is God's righteousness. If your desire is to be right with God, you must "put on Christ" (II Corinthians 5:21):

> *"For He hath made Him to be sin for us, who knew no sin; that we might be made the righteousness of God in Him."*

God is righteous, and He demands righteousness from every sinner. How? God, through the cross, has graciously provided that righteousness in the Person of the Lord Jesus Christ. It is important to remember that we cannot obtain righteousness on our own accord – neither by our holiness nor by our works. Righteousness comes only by the grace of the Lord. Daily, He sanctifies us and leads us into paths of righteousness. Our dependence upon Christ for righteousness is likened to a baby that relies totally on his/her mother for sustenance. The child is nurtured, and he/she grows and matures because of the mother's expressed love, care and dedication. We, too, are kept spiritually alive only through the righteousness of Christ. Our own righteousness is as filthy rags in His sight (Isaiah 64:6).

c.   He convicts man of judgment

The ministry of the Holy Spirit to the unsaved extends to convicting them of judgment, because the prince of this world is judged. Who is the prince of this world, and why is he judged? Once you determine just who he truly is, then the answer to the latter question should become obvious. The prince of this world is none other but Satan the devil, also known as the ruler of the world. Note that in no way does this limit or diminish the power and essence of God Almighty who is the Creator of the universe.

When Satan was thrown out of heaven for rebelling against God, he then became the unseen ruler of the world (John 12:31; 14:30; 16:11). Since then, Satan's preoccupation has been to control the people and nations of the world. Do you remember how it began back in the Garden of Eden? At that time, he succeeded in tricking Eve and robbing her and Adam of their legitimate ownership and rule over the earth (Revelation 12:9).

Also, do you recall in Luke chapter four, how Satan even tempted Jesus, but failed miserably in his attempt to get Christ to yield?

Today, all unsaved persons are inhabitants of Satan's kingdom. They are his slaves, and have joined with him to rebel against God. They have created enmity between themselves and God. The Bible declares that friendship with the world is enmity with God. The Holy Spirit seeks to judge the hearts of the unsaved and lead them to repentance.

The revelation of judgment to the unsaved by the Holy Spirit also involves:

i. The differences in lifestyles of the saved and the unsaved:

Every sinner will realize that there are clear differences between believers and unbelievers, when it comes to their lifestyles – and everything else. For instance, after I received Christ, my unsaved friends would always hide their cigarettes from me whenever I visited with them. I believe their action was a result of the conviction of the Holy Spirit. He makes the unbeliever unsecured and uncomfortable in the presence of the believer, in whose body He resides.

ii. The difference between light and darkness

Unbelievers being evil, are promoters of evil deeds. Their actions are carried out in darkness and in secret places. They are unable to come into the light to commit their deeds because of guilt or condemnation. Sadly, while they know their actions are wrong, they lack the willpower to resist temptations.

iii. The difference between God and Satan.

The Holy Spirit will reveal to the unsaved that God is a **GOOD** God, but the devil is bad, and that God is righteous, but Satan is evil. Here is the testimony of King Pharaoh in Exodus 9:27

> *"And Pharaoh sent, and called for Moses and Aaron, and said unto them, I have sinned this time: the LORD is righteous, and I and my people are wicked."*

iv. The difference between **GOOD** and **EVIL**

The Holy Spirit shows to unbelievers that there is a difference between what is good and what is evil. He reveals to them that good will last and evil will not. And so, every unbeliever knows that God will bless that which is good and punish that which is evil. This revelation leaves the unbeliever without any excuse (Romans 1:18, 19).

3. His ministry concerning the revelation of God's holiness

Unless God's holiness is displayed, it is sometimes difficult for one to come under true conviction. Isaiah as we know, was a mighty Old Testament prophet of the LORD. He cried out in repentance when he had a partial view of God's glory, or His holiness (Isaiah 6:1-7):

> *"In the year that King Uzziah died, I saw also the Lord sitting upon a throne, high and lifted up and his train filled the temple. Above it stood the seraphims: each one had six wings; with twain he covered his face, and with twain he covered his feet, and with twain he did fly. And one cried unto another, and said, Holy, holy, holy, is the LORD of host: The whole earth is full of His glory. And the posts of the door moved at the voice of him that cried, and the house was filled with smoke. Then said I, woe is me! For I am undone; because I am a man of unclean lips, and I dwell in the midst of a people with unclean lips: For mine eyes have* seen *the King, the LORD of hosts. Then, flew one of the Seraphims unto me, having a live coal in his hand, which he hath taken with the tongs from off the altar: And he laid it upon my mouth, and said, Lo, this hath touched thy lips; and thine iniquity is taken away, and thy sin is purged."*

Dear Reader, I urge you to see (perceive) the LORD for the glorious God He is. If not, you will not be able to see yourself clearly. I believe the clearest mirror that reflects your real self before the LORD is the mirror of His holiness.

At a time in my life while visiting Guinea in West Africa, I recall a testimony about a man who attended worship service under the influence of much alcohol. According to him, it was very difficult to understand the message at the beginning due to his confused state of mind. But somewhere in the middle of the sermon, the glory of the LORD was revealed to him, and he was instantly released from his intoxication.

In Acts 9:1-6, we read the story of Paul's conversion. Saul, as he was known by the Jews prior to his conversion, immediately surrendered to the voice of the Lord when he experienced His full glory with a blinding radiance on the Damascus road. Two major things could take place when God's glory is revealed to a sinner or a backslider.

i. The person responds in repentance and is blessed for the rest of his/her life.
ii. He/she rejects the glory of God and is condemned forever.
May this never be your portion, in Jesus' name!

4. His ministry concerning the revelation of man's sinfulness

At my conversion, I vividly remember that the primary reason I fell to my knees and cried out for mercy was my sinfulness. When I saw how dirty I was in the eyes of the Holy God, I was convicted. I believe many people are living in sin today because the eyes and heart of their understanding are still darkened. I pray that you will receive spiritual insight today, in Jesus' name.

5. His ministry concerning the revelation of Christ as the only remedy for man's salvation

Unfortunately, many Jews living in Israel at the time of the Lord Jesus did not believe He was the only Savior, because they lacked spiritual perception. (Some hold the same view today). Notwithstanding, a good number of them were convicted of their sin of unbelief while Peter preached on one occasion in Jerusalem (Acts chapter two). Under conviction, these believing Jews asked Peter and the rest of the apostles: "What shall we do?"

The Bible says that Peter, under the anointing of the Holy Spirit, said unto them:

> *"...Repent, and be baptized every one of you in the name of Jesus Christ for the remission of sins, and ye shall receive the gift of the Holy Ghost" (v. 38).*

> *"Then they that gladly received His word were baptized: and the same day there were added unto them about three thousand souls" (v. 41).*

Is the Holy Spirit still at work today? Certainly, yes! He is very busy in the world bringing people to Jesus through his mighty convicting power. Have you ever been under His conviction? If you have, please settle it with the Lord now. If you are still wondering, unsure of such a possibility, be assured that it is possible for you to come under conviction. The Spirit of God can reveal God's holiness to you; He is also able to reveal your sinful, helpless state and impress upon your heart the redemptive work Christ undertook on your behalf. The choice is clearly yours to respond positively to His convicting power or ignore it, but I urge you to swiftly heed. This is what is recorded in Acts 7:51:

> *"Ye stiffnecked and uncircumcised in hearts and ears, ye do always resist the Holy Ghost: as your fathers did, so do ye."*

It is evident from these passages that the possibility exists for someone under the conviction of the Holy Spirit to continuously rebel against God and to reject His offer of salvation.

In a nutshell, I have listed below instances in the Scriptures relative to the powerful ministry of the Holy Spirit in bringing conviction to the hearts of men/women:

1. The crowd at Pentecost (Acts 2:22, 23, 37)
2. The Ethiopian Eunuch (Acts 8:29-38)
3. Saul of Tarsus (Acts 9:1-6)
4. The Centurion and his household (Acts 10:44)
5. The Philippians Jailer (Acts 16:25-34)
6. A Governor named Felix (Acts 24: 24, 25)
7. King Agrippa (Acts 26: 23-28)
8. King David (II Samuel 12: 1-9)

The Holy Spirit does not only bring conviction to sinners, He also convicts the saints. In instances where believers compromise with sin or walk in disobedience, He convicts us. The Lord desires that we yield swiftly and consciously to the Spirit's conviction and repent. It is no mistake that sin puts believers out of fellowship with God, but the Holy Spirit always alerts us to this truth. Believers should never allow the enemy to lead them into darkness. Satan's intent is to blind us and make us unconscious of the truth. Certainly, I believe it is possible for you to find yourself in a state of denial and unrepentance, because you may not want to take responsibility for your wrongful acts against God and your fellowman. In such a situation, you may remain in your blindness and out of fellowship with God, if the veil is not removed. But if you yield to the Holy Spirit's promptings or guidance, then you have overcome the enemy.

On the other hand, there are those who choose only to be defiant. They live comfortably in gross disobedience, resulting into a lifestyle of habitual ungodliness and carnality. Their salvation then becomes questionable.

We have already read about the sins of adultery and murder committed by King David. He did everything to continue to cover up his sins until Nathan the prophet revealed them to him through the voice of the Spirit. After this, David repented and was restored (II Samuel 12:1-9).

Have you ever found yourself in a similar situation? Like David, have you ever been confronted about a wrongful act? What was your reaction? Did you become offended or did you repent and ask God's forgiveness? Whenever you are reminded or convicted of sin, your love for God and your humility in His Holy presence should always bring you to a place of complete submission and surrender. Arguments and self-denials are unnecessary. They will undeniably lead to more rebellion against God. The Bible says in I John1:9:

> *"If we confess our sins, He is faithful and just to forgive us of our sins, and to cleanse us from all unrighteousness."*

Remember the warning of Solomon from his wisdom diary: *"He that covereth his sin shall not prosper: but whoso shall confesseth and forsaketh them shall have mercy"* (Proverb 28:13). Please act upon these words.

6. His daily ministry of salvation in the world
   a. He is the Chief Propagator of the Gospel (Luke 8:5-15; Romans 1:16; 10: 14-17; I Corinthians 1:18-24).
   b. He is the Chief Agent of conviction to people (Zechariah 12: 10; John 16: 7-11; I Corinthians 14:24).
   c. He is the great source of regeneration. He gives birth to all that come to Jesus.

d. He is the glorious Holy Sanctifier (Romans 15:16; II Thessalonians 2:13; I Peter 1:3). He sets people apart for God's holy use.

7. His ministry concerning believers
   a. The Holy Spirit gives birth to all believers. Without the Holy Spirit no spiritual birth on earth can take place. There can be no connection with the kingdom of God, irrespective of one's traditional and cultural background or religious orientation.

In the world today, many claim that there exists several ways to attain salvation in God's realm of life. For the Muslims, salvation means praying five times a day, giving alms to the poor, and making pilgrimages to Mecca every year. What about our Lorma tribe in Liberia and Guinea?

Our tradition demands that one shows respect towards elders; display good and acceptable character, follow cultural rituals, refrain from practicing witchcraft and harming innocent people in any way or form; and show hospitality towards strangers. Note that when it comes to witchcraft practices, the village elders only pretended to advocate against it; nonetheless they compromised their "principles" by practicing this wickedness. These and many other misconceptions not mentioned here are all mere opinions of men. They are indicators of self-centeredness, carnality and/or absolute rebellion – the standards and values that are used to determine their perception of God, and the extent they believe they must go to find Him and gain His acceptance.

Our God is a God of absolute integrity. He has set forth His own standards in His Word. Without bias, these Holy standards are written for all who desire to join His Family and to live a God-conscious life. In John's Gospel 3:3-8, the Lord Jesus said unto Nicodemus:

"Verily, verily, I say unto thee, Except a man be born again, he cannot see the kingdom of God" (v. 3).

That which is born of the flesh is flesh; and that which is born of the Spirit is spirit" *(v.6)*.

i.   This new birth in Christ gives us access to God as full fleshed members of His Holy Family (Ephesians 2:11-13). We are automatically placed into a new position of son-ship, as explained in John 1:12.

ii.   We become new creatures in Christ Jesus (II Corinthians 5:17).

iii. Our connection to God makes us citizens of Heaven ("Heavenians"), members of the highest royal family, not just citizens of our various earthly nations.

iv.   We have complete and immediate availability to the voice of God:

"My sheep hear my voice, and I know them, and they follow me:" (John 10:27).

v.   We have passed from death to life. Spiritual death no more has authority over our lives:

"Verily, verily, I say unto you, He that heareth my word, and believeth on him that sent me, hath everlasting life, and shall not come into condemnation; but is passed from death unto life" (John 5:24).

The new birth in Christ brings us into union with God Almighty. It gives us access into God's class of life. We become God's first family members on the earth and we are now royal and blessed forever.

vi.   We have been translated from darkness into light, and delivered from the realm and power of Satan to that of God. **"Who hath delivered** *us from the power of darkness, and hath translated us into the kingdom of his dear Son:"* (Colossians 1:13).

vii. We have been elevated to the center of all power (Ephesians 2:4-6). Our ascension to this throne along with Christ speaks of our uplifted position of glory and honor in Him. This throne by far excels all others; it is ascended far beyond the kingdom of darkness.

viii. We also enjoy the *"blessing"* of our forefather Abraham (Galatians 3:13, 14). It is this whole package of *"blessing"* under the Abrahamic Covenant that first enabled us to be passed from spiritual death to spiritual life, bringing along its benefits of enrichments, abundance and fruitfulness (III John 2; II Corinthians 8:9).

b. He baptizes the believer into the Body of Christ

"For as many of you as have been baptized into Christ have put on Christ" (Galatians 3:27).

During this mystical event, the Holy Spirit merges the believer into the Body of Christ. The Body of Christ is composed of all those that are born again, whether in heaven or on the earth. For the believer here on the earth, he/she then becomes one of the functioning parts of the universal Body of Christ, which is the Church of the living God.

c. The Holy Spirit indwells us

The Holy Spirit comes to live within us, to make us His living temple. What a privilege and a blessing! Our bodies are hosts to the *ALMIGHTY ONE, our REVERED CREATOR*, through the presence of the Third Person of the Trinity (Holy Spirit). When we compare this aspect of the Holy Spirit's ministry to the Ark of the Covenant where God's presence dwelt in Old Testament times, we make the following observations from the Scriptures:

> ***"Know ye not that ye are the temple of God, and that the Spirit of God dwelleth in you?"*** (I Corinthians 3:16).

> ***"And I will pray the Father, and He shall give you another Comforter, that he may abide with you forever;"*** (John 14:16).

With His presence, we are properly equipped with divine power and authority to ascend to the throne to rule over the earth. Let me individualize this; I trust you, too, would do the same. "I, Anthony F. B. Tarnue, carry in me the HOLY ONE, under whose anointed authority Satan trembles and demons flee. The Lord who has power over death, to whom all heavenly and earthly things submit, all knees bow, every tongue confess, and to whom all are accountable." Blessed be His Holy name, Amen!

d. He seals every believer

The Holy Spirit places a mark on everyone He births. This is a mark of heavenly distinction, an evidence of the believer's internal and external security in the Lord.

This means that we are sealed both inwardly and outwardly by the Holy Spirit who, Himself, is that seal. To possess this high level of security indicates that the believer is protected both spiritually and physically forever:

> ***"Who hath also sealed us, and given the earnest of the Spirit in our hearts"*** (II Corinthians 1:22).

e. He desires to baptize every believer with Himself and with fire (Acts 2:1-4):

"And when the day of Pentecost was fully come, they were all with one accord in one place. And suddenly there came a sound from heaven as of a rushing mighty wind, and it filled all the house where they were sitting. And there appeared unto them cloven tongues like as of fire, and it sat upon each of them. And they were all filled with the Holy Ghost, and began to speak with other tongues, as the Spirit gave them utterance."

There is a Spirit *"within"* and a Spirit *"upon"*. When one becomes genuinely born again or regenerated; the Spirit of God (Holy Spirit) immediately enters and dwells within that person. This is, of course, the new birth, the initial blessing everyone who is born of God receives (I Corinthians 12:13).

Subsequently, when the believer is baptized in the Holy Spirit, the individual's regenerated spirit rises up to overshadow that person's entire personality (Acts 2:1-4).

By receiving the baptism in the Spirit, the person enters into a new and higher dimension of God's blessings and favor.

Unlike the baptism with the Spirit that is a solitary (one time) experience by virtue of the new birth, the filling (baptism in the Spirit) is not limited to only a particular time or place. It may be experienced over and over again, as the Holy Spirit desires. Some refer to this as the second "blessing;" others say it is the "endowment of power" for ministry. Overall, this experience is the fulfillment of God's promises, as mentioned in Joel 2:28, 29.

It is a fact that in God's work of salvation, the important role of the Holy Spirit cannot be over emphasized. We are born into God's Kingdom by the Spirit (John 3:5), and we are baptized into the Body of Christ Jesus by the same Spirit's power (Acts 2:1-4, 4:31; I Corinthians 12:13):

> *"For by one Spirit are we all baptized into one body, whether we be Jews or Gentiles, whether we be bond or free; and have been all made to drink into one Spirit" (I Corinthians 12:13).*

Here are other citations concerning experiences of the baptism in the Holy Spirit with fire: Acts 8:14-17; Acts 10:14-16; Acts 19:1-6.

Contrasting the Spirit "within" with the Spirit "upon," there are obvious differences. The Spirit "upon" was a manifestation of God's Spirit in the Old Testament Dispensation. The Spirit of the LORD occasionally came upon God's messengers or chosen, to help them accomplish a particular duty, or to enable them to fulfill their calling, mission or assignment. Whereas in the New Testament Dispensation, the Holy Spirit now takes up resident in all believers. In Him we live, in Him we move, and in Him we have our being.

f.   The Holy Spirit desires to ANOINT every believer for ministry (I John 2: 20, 27):

> *"But ye have an unction from the Holy One, and ye know all things" (v. 20).*

> *"But the anointing which ye have received of Him abideth in you, and ye need not that any man teach you: but as the same anointing teaches you of all things, and is truth, and is no lie, and even as it hath taught you, ye shall abide in him" (v. 27).*

In the Old Testament, everyone whom God chose or used to carry out a specific assignment (Isaiah 45:1) had to first have His anointing.

In fact, God's anointing was limited to prophets (I Kings 19:16), priests (Exodus 40:15; Leviticus 21:10), and kings (I Samuel 10:1; 16:13). These kings and priests were ceremoniously anointed with oil, both as a sign of official appointment to office, and as a symbol of God's power upon them. Without His anointing, they could not function in accordance with His divine plan.

The anointing, then, is essentially the power of God in manifestation. Today it is a certain measure or level of God's presence upon an individual. The Scriptures illustrate three measures or levels of the anointing.

1. There is the *"WELL"* level of the anointing:

> *"But whosoever drinketh of the water that I shall give him shall never thirst; but the water that I shall give him shall be in him a well of water springing up into everlasting life"* (John 4:14).

At birth in Christ, a certain level of God's presence comes to abide in the child of God. We must remember, however, that a well is controlled by climatic and weather conditions. For instance, the hot summer temperatures could cause most wells to dry up. But during the seasons of rain or snow they are filled up again. At this level, the believer has not yet experienced the baptism in the Holy Spirit because he/she still lacks the fullness of the Spirit; that believer has yet to attain the fullest level of lifestyle that God desires.

Most times under the control of his/her flesh, the individual may lack the spiritual energy to flow with God at all times. Therefore, every individual must strive never to remain at this level. He/she must desire to enter into God's fullness through the baptism of the Holy Spirit.

2. There is the *"RIVER"* Level of the Anointing

First of all, let us examine the characteristics of a river:

a.   A river flows (unlike the well that remains still).

b.   A river carries people or things.

c.   A river has a force that may be difficult to stop.

d.   A river travels at a far distance.

e.   A river gives life.

By now, we do know that the river spoken of here figuratively describes the baptism in the Holy Spirit, according to John 7:38,39. We have these Words from the lips of our Lord Jesus:

> *"He that believeth on me, as the scripture hath said, out of his belly shall flow rivers of living water. (But this spake he of the Spirit, which they that believe on him should receive: for the Holy Ghost was not yet given; because that Jesus was not yet glorified.)"*

At the baptism in the Holy Spirit, it is God's will for the life of the believer to continue its transformation process and not to remain at the well level. Once at the river level, the believer's life flows to others by the power of the Holy Spirit already resident within the believer. He/she accomplishes this through the use of the acquired gifts of the Spirit. The believer's lifestyle is then characterized by color and attractiveness through the fruit of his/her regenerated spirit (Galatians 5:22-23).

At the river level, there is a divine force working in the believer's life. It cannot be hindered by any human effort, or by any circumstance or situation, not even the worst form of persecution. Why? Because he/she is covered under the great anointing of the Holy Spirit. As the river impacts every object in its path, so does the power of the Holy Spirit allow the life of the believer to overflow and to meaningfully alter the lives of others.

Just as the river nourishes and maintains the life of every living thing in its surroundings, so does the believer, by the power of the Holy Ghost. As the river transports objects along its path, so is the power of the Holy Spirit manifested in those who allow Him to overflow their lives (Ezekiel 47: 3 – 5; Joel 2:28, 29).

3.   There is the *"RAIN"* Level of the Anointing

Of a surety, the anointing is measureable in the life of every believer. I have observed that some sons and daughters of God are more anointed than others. At certain times in our own Christian journey, we may experience a higher filling of the anointing than at other times. On such occasions, the Holy Spirit is evidently present to use us to display His power and to edify others through the use of any of the gifts of the Spirit. Whether by word of wisdom or knowledge; whether by the gift of faith or healing; whether by the working of miracles; whether by prophecy, tongues and interpretations, or whether by the discerning of spirits, it is through the anointed ministry of the Holy Spirit that all these manifestations are possible (I Corinthians 12).

Also at the rain level of the anointing, everyone and everything around the believer is affected by this level of God's presence in the same way natural rain descends and affects its surroundings. Rain pours unselectively; it has no preferences.

Below are some great manifestations of the rain level of God's presence in the Scriptures. You will observe that without praying or laying on of hands, only the presence of God upon the apostles in turn impacted the lives of others:

"And by the hands of the apostles were many signs and wonders wrought among the people; Insomuch that they brought forth the sick into the streets, and laid them on beds and couches, that at

***the least the shadow of Peter passing by might overshadow some
of them. There came also a multitude out of the cities round
about unto Jerusalem, bringing sick folks, and them which were
vexed with unclean spirits: and they were healed every one"***
(Acts 5:12,15,16).

Under this unction, the believer becomes immovable, unbeatable, and
unstoppable against any attack of the devil. He/she walks under the cloud of
God's glory. Paul at one time came under this level of God's anointing; even the
prison doors could not stop the move of God's power (Acts 16:25-31; 19:11, 12).

***"And God wrought special miracles by the hands of Paul: So
that from his body were brought unto the sick handkerchiefs or
aprons, and the diseases departed from them, and the evil spirits
went out of them"*** (Acts 9:11-12).

*[Prayer]: LORD, I desire that this level of your presence rests upon me for
the expansion of your kingdom worldwide, and only for your glory, in
Jesus' name. By faith I desire it, in the name of Jesus my LORD, Amen.*

The baptism, the filling and the anointing of the Holy Spirit in the
lives of believers are all given to glorify God in these ways:

1. To help believers live above sin and walk in righteousness.
2. To enable believers proclaim the Gospel to all nations, and make
   disciples of them for God's kingdom (Mathew 28:18-20; Mark
   16:15-18).
3. To give believers the ability to manifest in the gifts of the Holy Spirit
   (I Corinthians 12:28; Romans 12:6-8).
4. To empower believers to function properly in one or more of the
   fivefold ministry gifts (Ephesians 4:11-12).

5.   To signify believers' authority over Satan, his cohorts and all his works:

> *"Behold, I give unto you power to tread on serpents and scorpions, and over all the power of the enemy: and nothing shall by any means hurt you"* (Luke 10:19).

The dominion that Adam lost at the fall has been redeemed and restored at Calvary. The believer is no longer a slave to the devil but a master in Christ over him. If you are a true Christian, you should never be afraid of Satan and his followers. We are more than conquerors through Christ our King over the kingdom of darkness.

h. How can one experience the baptism in the Holy Spirit? The baptism in the Holy Spirit or the receiving of the Holy Ghost is an experience subsequent to salvation. Every born again believer must desire to be baptized in the Holy Spirit.

Is there any difference between the Spirit at the new birth and the Spirit at baptism? Yes, from Biblical proofs there is a vast difference. The Spirit at the new birth is received initially at conversion, while the Spirit at baptism is the endowment of power. Let's look at Acts 8:12, 13:

> *"But when they believed Philip preaching the things concerning the kingdom of God, and the name of Jesus Christ, they were baptized, both men and women. Then Simon himself believed also: and when he was baptized, he continued with Philip, and wondered, beholding the miracles and signs which were done."*

According to these verses, Philip the evangelist, experienced a great move of God in Samaria when he preached Jesus; many were saved and delivered from evil spirits (8:7, 8).

However, the apostles in the Jerusalem Church did not believe that the new converts had received the "whole package," as it pertained to the Holy Spirit. So they sent Peter and John to release upon the Samaritans the special grace that had come upon them (the apostles) – which grace was the laying on of hands upon the Samaritan believers – that they might also receive the baptism in the Holy Spirit:

> *"Now when the apostles which were at Jerusalem heard that Samaria had received the word of God, they sent unto them Peter and John: Who, when they were come down, prayed for them, that they might receive the Holy Ghost: (For as yet he was fallen upon none of them: only they were baptized in the name of the Lord Jesus). Then laid they their hands on them, and they received the Holy Ghost" (vv. 14-17).*

Simon the sorcerer also requested to receive the power to lay hands, that people might receive the Holy Spirit (Acts 8:18,19). This was obviously denied by the apostles. But I believe that for a sorcerer to have made such a request, even though for the wrong motive, points to the fact that the possibility does exist for believers to be baptized in the Holy Spirit.

1. The Baptism in the Holy Spirit is a **FREE GIFT** promised to every believer by the Lord Jesus Christ, the ***GREAT CAPTAIN** of our salvation*.

a. Joel 2:28-29:

> *"And it shall come to pass afterward, that I will pour out my spirit upon all flesh; and your sons and your daughters shall prophesy, your old men shall dream dreams, your young men*

shall see visions: And also upon the servants and upon the handmaids in those days will I pour out my spirit."

The gift of the Holy Spirit is very important in the life of every believer. Our maturity in the Lord, as well as our productivity in His service is dependent upon His empowerment. The pouring out of God's Spirit is not limited only to a particular group of people. It is promised to everyone in all the world – that is, all who know Him. It is not restricted to color, nationality, creed, status or age.

It is promised to our sons and daughters who receive the Spirit that a measure of the gift of prophesy is theirs. Prophecy has two levels:

1. At this level, it means to predict the future, and to communicate future happenings in the present.
2. At the other level, prophecy carries the idea of edification, exaltation and comfort. This type of prophetic ministry is to encourage, to exalt and to provide comfort to the Body of Christ.

Pertaining to the first level, visions can be analyzed in light of:

1. Open visions – this is where your physical sight is suspended so that the spirit world is revealed to you through your spiritual eyes.
2. Close visions – these types of visions are closely related to dreams, in that while being deeply asleep, your human spirit travels and has the ability to view the spirit world. Future events are then revealed to you for your own benefit as well as for the benefit of others.
3. The revelation of your purpose on earth. This can be revealed to you by way of an open vision, through a close vision, or from your human mind. This is more or less a mental picture relative to your mission on earth.

To the old men, the prophecy points out that they will dream dreams, in the context of another level of revelation. Many times God has revealed deep secrets to people that possess this gift. A fine example is the young man Joseph. His divine destiny in life was revealed unto him in dreams (Genesis 37:1-5).

b.   The Lord Jesus promised to pray to the Father to send this precious gift:

"And I will pray the Father, and he shall give you another Comforter, that he may abide with you forever; Even the Spirit of truth; whom the world cannot receive, because it seeth Him not, neither knoweth him: but ye know him; for He dwelleth with you, and shall be in you" (John 14:16-17).

c.   The Master told His first disciples to tarry for the promise of the Holy Spirit:

"And, behold, I send the promise of my Father upon you: but tarry ye in the city of Jerusalem, until ye be endued with power from on high" (Luke 24:49).

d.   The promise of the Holy Spirit is for ***ALL***, including your biological and extended families, your friends, Jews and Gentiles alike, as well as the bond and the free:

"Then Peter said unto them, Repent, and be baptized every one of you in the name of Jesus Christ for the remission of sins, and ye shall receive the gift of the Holy Ghost. For the promise is unto you, and to your children, and to all that are afar off, even as many as the Lord our God shall call" (Acts 2:38, 39).

2. The baptism in the Holy Spirit has many infallible proofs

a. The promise was first fulfilled when the Holy Spirit came upon the 120 disciples in Jerusalem (Acts 2:1-4).

Friend, God is not a man that He should lie, neither the Son of Man that He should repent. Has He not said it and shall He not do it? Has He not spoken and shall He not make it good? He said it, and He did it after 40 days!

b. The believers in Samaria became filled or baptized in the Holy Spirit subsequent to salvation (8:14-17).
c. In approximately 10 years, the believers in Cornelius' house received the promise (Acts 10:44-46).

Note that the baptism in the Holy Spirit, which began in Jerusalem with the 120 disciples, comprised of only Jewish believers. The believers in Samaria that received the baptism were Jewish proselytes (half Jews and half Gentiles). As for Cornelius, the Roman Centurion and his household, they were the first Gentiles to receive this glorious gift when it was extended to the Gentile world (Acts10:44-46). These events took place as the Lord had promised.

d. Twenty years after the Day of Pentecost, the Ephesian believers received the Holy Spirit (Acts19:2,3,6): *He said unto them, Have ye received the Holy Ghost since ye believed? And they said unto him, We have not so much as heard whether there be any Holy Ghost. And he said unto them, Unto what then were ye baptized? And they said, Unto John's baptism" (vv. 2-3).*

> **"And when Paul had laid his hands upon them, the Holy Ghost
> came on them; and they spake with tongues, and prophesied"
> (v. 6).**

e. Paul, once a rebel against the Church of God, had received the Holy
    Spirit's baptism and was then laying hands on believers to receive the
    same power from God. You can read about the detailed account of his
    encounter with the Holy Spirit from Acts 9:3-6.

3. Here are the steps you must follow to receive the baptism in the Holy
   Spirit:
   a. You must be born again (Mark 16:15, 16; John 3:3-7).
   b. You must believe what God's Word says – that this gift is also for
       you (Acts 2:38, 39).
   c. You must receive this gift by faith (Hebrew 11:6).
   d. Begin to give thanks to God for your glorious gift.

As a point of significance, we must again recognize the Holy Spirit's
wonderful work in regenerating every believing sinner that comes to Jesus.
From our physical realm of life, it is impossible for a cat to give birth to
a puppy. A cat can only beget a kitten. From the vegetable kingdom, an
apple tree can only produce apple fruits, while a mango tree will only bring
forth mango fruits. This is an unchangeable law that applies both to the
spiritual and the physical, that *"like begets like."* Therefore, spirit can only
give birth to spirit. In John 3:3-7, we have Jesus' Words to us:

> **"Jesus answered and said unto him, Verily, verily, I say unto
> thee, Except a man be born again, he cannot see the kingdom
> of God" (v. 3).**

Nicodemus saith unto Him, *"How can a man be born when he is old? Can he enter the second time into his mother's womb, and be born?"* (v. 4).

Jesus answered, *"Verily, verily, I say unto thee, Except a man be born of water and of the Spirit, he cannot enter into the kingdom of God"* (v. 5).

"That which is born of the flesh is flesh; and that which is born of the Spirit is spirit" (v. 6).

"Marvel not that I said unto thee, Ye must be born again" (v. 7).

Whenever a person accepts Jesus Christ as Savior and Lord, his/her sins are forgiven, and God's nature, through the power of the Holy Spirit, is imparted into that believer's spirit. As a result, the spirit of the new Christian again takes on the life of God that Adam had lost at the fall. That supernatural act then allows the believer's spirit-man to become alive from sin unto God. This is a great mystery.

Beloved, have you experienced this kind of life? Are you born again? If so, what are your evidences? Please read II Corinthians 5:17 and 6:14-18. There are many mighty mysteries of the Holy Spirit for you to encounter, as you open up yourself to Him.

CHAPTER SIX

THE SOURCE OF OUR SALVATION

A. The Word of God

The Word of God is the principle source of salvation for all. There is nothing in existence in this world today without a Word being spoken by the LORD. In Hebrews 11:3 we have these Words: "Through faith we understand that the worlds were framed by the Word of God, so that things which are seen were not made of things which do appear." We have even seen that when it comes to the regeneration of our human spirits, it takes the same Word of God to bring back the life of God into our spirits. In Romans 10:13, 17 the Bible says:

> *"For whosoever shall call upon the name of the Lord shall be saved. So then faith cometh by hearing, and hearing by the word of God."*

Beloved, pending the release of God's Word from His holy mouth, creation was not in view. Except the Word is echoed in the ears of sinners for their hearing, salvation for them will be far from reality. It was a necessity for the Gospel message to be heard by all who have been saved today, whether the Word came from a man or an angel. We know that before the Lord Jesus Christ departed planet earth He spoke saying:

"... Go ye into the entire world, and preach the gospel to every creature, He that believeth and is baptized shall be saved; but he that believeth not shall be damned." And they went forth, and preached everywhere, the Lord working with them, and confirming the word with signs following. Amen" (Mark 16: 15, 16 and 20).

The proclamation of the Gospel of the kingdom is a top priority to God. It is paramount that this message reaches the hearing of the lost in order to give them the opportunity to be saved. Cornelius claimed to be very religious; but nothing could have saved him until he heard the convicting Words through the apostle Peter. The instruction to "Go" is for all believers, not only pastors and evangelists. First, you must allow the Word of God to be manifested in your lifestyle – this is a powerful way of witnessing. With the help of the Holy Spirit, you will gradually grow and develop boldness in presenting Christ to the lost. You have the authority in you to do so. As a light to the dark world, you are a city on the hill that cannot be hidden. You illuminate and draw the attention of the lost, not to yourself, but to the light and Savior of the world, Jesus Christ (John 8:12). He lives in you and you live by Him. Without His presence, you could never shine. In fact, He was the very light that delivered you from the power of darkness that once controlled your life. Now, your life is welcoming, inviting and infectious. You cannot avoid being noticed because your light shines with the love of Christ; and this is exactly the purpose for which you were created: to radiate and spread the light of the Gospel to the lost. The Lord is depending on you.

The forces of darkness are facing tremendous distress. You continue to bombard them, making inroads into their territory to depopulate it and to populate God's kingdom. As you gain the lost for Christ, you vigorously and unashamedly follow the example of the Apostle Paul who declared in Romans 1:16 that He was not ashamed of the Gospel; for it is the power of God for salvation to everyone who believes... You are confident that the same Gospel that saved you from hell's destruction can transform the worse of sinners. Here is an example of the power of God's Word when released.

It was in the year 1980 back home in Liberia when I encountered this experience. One night as I was driving home, I came across a military personnel standing in the middle of the highway. He hailed me and asked for a ride. Reluctantly I consented, since he was heading in my direction. As we rode together I heard the voice of the Holy Spirit saying, "Preach the Gospel to him." My first reaction was disobedience to the Spirit; there was much suspicion surrounding this man's strange behavior. However, the voice continued to urge me to witness the love of Jesus to him, and I finally yielded.

Afterwards, he asked if I were a fortune teller or a physic because according to him, I had just saved the lives of three persons. I became very curious and asked him to reveal the details of his story. Sadly, he narrated the unfortunate incident about discovering his wife was cheating on him, and that she had left home to be with her lover. He said he had therefore decided to kill both of them and then take his own life. He confessed that upon hearing the Gospel message, something had moved his heart, and he had changed his mind about proceeding with his plan to commit the murder-suicide. Best of all, that dear man expressed a desire to give his life to Christ. What a moment; this was astounding!

Beloved, this story presents many lessons. Most importantly, it reminds us that believers must always be able to discern the voice or guidance of the Holy Spirit in using them to witness the Word at every single opportunity. Our duty is to obey, and the Holy Spirit's convicting power will do the rest.

B. The Blood of Jesus

There are three things to consider under this discussion:

1. The lamb – this domestic animal played a primary role in the sacrificial system of the Jewish people: during the annual Passover celebrations (Exodus 12:1-36) and in the daily sacrifices of Israel (Leviticus 14:12-21), a lamb was used for these sacrifices. In the Old Testament, the lamb was, of course, a type of Jesus who did manifest as the sacrificial Lamb of the world in the New Testament era.
2. Sacrifices and offerings – are physical elements the Jewish people brought to God as expressions of their devotion to Him, for thanksgiving purposes, or to seek His forgiveness.

Please observe that this sacrificial system involved various types of sacrifices including burnt offering (Leviticus 1; 6:8-13); meat offering (Leviticus 2); fellowship or peace offering (3; 7:11-21); sin offering (6:24-30); guilt offering (4; 5) and drink offering (23:13; Numbers 28,29).

The use of animals for sacrifices reminds me about similar rituals that were done in my village when I was yet an unsaved young man. Our tradition depicted that animals such as lambs, goats and roosters be used for such sacrifices. They were carried out with pride and dignity. When they were performed during periods of tribal wars, the sacrifices were intended to appease the spirits of the ancestors to gain victory over our enemies. For the committal of gross "sins" or wrong doings by village elders, similar sacrifices were made. There was a compelling feeling to seek "good fortune." Being spiritually blind without the slightest knowledge of the Word, we were convinced that "salvation" from "sin" depended on the will and pleasure of our ancestors' spirits.

Like Israel, the village "priests" served as the mediator between the villagers and the spirit world. They presented all the villagers' requests to the ancestors.

Let me narrate to you a true story told to me by a pastor who once went through a horrific experience while living in the village as a young man.

He claimed that the entire clan was engaged in idol worship, and one of those idols was a very large snake that lived in a river near his village. Once, he was taken to the bank of the river and presented to the snake as a mediator. He was encouraged to be brave because if their sacrifice of a white rooster was accepted, the snake would then emerge out of the water and wrap itself around him. As anticipated, amidst his fears and anxieties, this was exactly what transpired. Meanwhile, the rest of the villagers began to sing, dance and make merry. They were pleased that their so-called "god" had accepted their sacrifice and their newly appointment "priest."

The pastor explained further that after the ceremony, the snake continued to appear and to wrap itself around him at night, perhaps as an indication of communion and fellowship. However, he said it was very difficult for him to sleep with such a monster and yet live a happy productive life.

Not knowing any better, he revealed that he sought the assistance of a number of witch doctors, to no avail. Finally, his deliverance from the power of darkness came when a missionary visited his village and presented Christ, the Lamb of God to him. The power of God proved exceedingly greater than the power of demons, witches and wizards.

The slaughter of a lamb for each individual family at the Passover in Egypt only brought about temporary salvation from bondage for the Israelites (Exodus 12). Back in Israel, all the sacrifices that were made at the annual Passover and Day of Atonement ceremonies were still insufficient and ineffectual. The daily sacrifices of the Israelites did not bring any permanent solution to their sin problem either.

Obviously, the animal sacrifices and idol worship that are continuously carried out today around the world have never worked, and will certainly not be sufficient to solve the problem of sin. Hebrews 9:22 tells us that without the shedding of blood, there is no remission or forgiveness of sin.

Isaac is also seen as a type of Christ mainly in relation to him being an only child – a child of promise from God to Abraham and Sarah who was born in their ripe old ages (Genesis 17:17; 21:5). Abraham's faith was tested and proven when he believed God, even at the last moment to his slaughtering of Isaac as a sacrificial offering, that the Lord would provide the appropriate animal to be sacrificed (22:1-19). Isaac was not slaughtered; but his sacrificed life would never have sufficed (Genesis 22:11-13):

> *"And the angel of the LORD called unto him out of heaven, and said, Abraham, Abraham: and he said: Here am I. And He said, Lay not thine hand upon the lad, neither do thou anything unto him: for now I know that thou fearest God, seeing thou hast not withheld thy son, thine only son from me. And Abraham lifted up his eyes, and looked, and behold behind him a ram caught in a thicket by his horns: and Abraham went and took the ram, and offered him up for a burnt offering in the stead of his son."*

My friend, any sacrifice outside of Christ's is not acceptable in the sight of God. Forgiveness of sin is impossible without the blood of Jesus. Under the Old Covenant, the blood of animals did not really wash away the sins of the Old Testament believers. Animal sacrifices only covered their sins from God's holiness. During the time of father Abraham, it was acceptable for one lamb to die for the life of one person.

3. The blood of Jesus offers salvation at three levels:

a. The blood at the level of protection. If you believe in it, the blood of Jesus will protect you from any evil. When God executed judgment upon the Egyptians, He used the method of the blood at the Passover to save Israel.

"And the blood shall be to you for a token upon the houses where you are: and when I see the blood I will pass over you, and the plague shall not be upon you to destroy you, when I smite the land of Egypt" (Exodus 12:1-13).

In this story, the lamb that was sacrificed and its blood sprung on the door posts of the Israelites was actually a type of Christ, God's Lamb to come. The safest place in Egypt for protection at that time was in the house where the lamb's blood was sprinkled. What about now? Your safest place to abide is right under the blood of Jesus. When the end of the world comes, and the judgment of the Lord strikes the world, you will be in great danger if you don't have the mark of the blood of Jesus upon your life.

b. The blood at the level of deliverance. Having been under bondage for 430 years in Egypt, Israel lost its freedom to the new pharaoh who did not know Joseph. Added to this, they also lost their dignity, their sense of value, their human rights and their wealth. God sent nine plagues for their freedom, but pharaoh refused. However, when the blood of the lamb was shed on behalf of Israel, pharaoh's power was broken. Israel obtained their liberty, and their dignity was restored.

c. The blood at the level of redemption. At this stage, the blood of the lamb did not only take Israel out of Egypt, but it also took Egypt out of them. That is, the blood redeemed Israel from Egypt to God and from slavery to freedom. As a result of the wonderful working power of the blood on behalf of Israel, many remarkable things happened, among which were the release of God's favor and glory upon them, as well as their increase in wealth (Exodus 12:35, 36; 13:21, 22).

C. The Triune God

The source of everyone's salvation is from ***GOD THE FATHER, GOD THE SON, and GOD THE HOLY SPIRIT – The THREE in ONE.***

1. God the FATHER as our source of salvation

   "Every good gift and every perfect gift is from above, and cometh down from the Father of lights, with whom is no variableness, neither shadow of turning. Of His own will begat He us with the word of truth, that we should be a kind of firstfruits of His creatures" (James 1:17-18).

   As Creator of the universe, God is the great designer and initiator of our salvation. He is the source of all things good and pleasant, all things glorious and beautiful, and all things great and perfect. He accomplished this for all believers, and He can do the same for you if you are not saved. He holds in His hands the highest power and hope that secures your salvation (Romans 10:13):

   "For whosoever shall call upon the name of the Lord shall be saved."

2. God the Son as our source of salvation

   In John 14:6, the Lord Jesus said: *"... I am the way, the truth and the life: no man cometh unto the Father, but by me."* There is no other way, no other truth, no other life outside of Christ. Although many people hold claims to several other avenues and so-called doctrines, we absolutely uphold the truth contained in the Word of God that there is only ***ONE WAY, ONE TRUTH*** and ***ONE LIFE***, the LORD JESUS! In Acts of the Apostles, we are told by the Holy Spirit through Peter, "***Neither is there salvation in any other: for there is none other name under heaven given among men, whereby we must be saved***" (Acts 4:12).

Anything outside the perimeter of Christ is dung, a waste of time, a deception and a plain lie from the pit of hell. Listen, the Bible says, at the mouth of two or three witnesses shall every word be established! The Father is the first witness. In Matthew 1:21, God proclaimed through the angel: ***"And she shall bring forth a son and thou shalt call His name Jesus: For He shall save His people from their sins."*** God is saying here that the solution to your sin problem is Christ Jesus, His loving Son. If you reject this revelation, true hope will definitely be unattainable. Without the hope that Christ gives, every other hope is false hope. It will eventually lead you to destruction. Therefore repent! Turn to the truth and be saved. The Son (Jesus Christ) bore a powerful second witness of Himself when He declared in John's Gospel that He was the only Way to salvation. In union with Him, God the Father and God the Holy Spirit also bear this witness. The three are inseparable, having been together before the foundations of the world. Do you bear witness of Jesus Christ as your Lord and Savior?

From the Day of Pentecost till now and forever, the Holy Spirit has and will continue to bear witness in the hearts of people that God is right, and that Jesus the Savior of the world is indeed the only Way.

3.   God the ***SPIRIT*** as our source of salvation

The Holy Spirit of God is God's agent on the earth today, executing His plan of salvation in the lives of all people. He reveals Jesus as the True Savior. He convicts sinners of their sins and points them to Jesus for their salvation. He is responsible to transport the new birth package into the hearts of all believing sinners. He opens people's eyes to see the holiness of God, the sinfulness of their own lives, and guides them into repentance (John 16:7; Acts 2:37, 38). Is God speaking to you today? Are you listening? Have you responded?

CHAPTER SEVEN

WHAT MUST I DO TO BE SAVED?

One of the most important questions people in today's world usually ask is, "What must I do to be saved?" This question has been asked since the work of redemption began. I have observed time and time again, that there comes a certain phase in the lives of unbelievers and backsliders, when they finally hit a brick wall or rock bottom in their "search" for successful living – when everything else has failed, and they have run out of "steam," out of options, and out of hope – only then do they preoccupy themselves to finding out how to escape their predicaments. In Acts 16: 27-31, the jailer came to his end, and asked the all-too-familiar question:

"And the keeper of the prison awaking out of his sleep, and seeing the prison doors open, he drew out his sword, and would have killed himself, supposing that the prisoners had been fled. But Paul cried with a loud voice, saying, Do thyself no harm: for we are all here. Then he called for a light, and sprang in, and came trembling, and fell down before Paul and Silas, And brought them out, and said, Sirs, what must I do to be saved?" Well, the answer to this question is found right in verse 31: *"And they said, Believe on the Lord Jesus Christ, and thou shalt be saved, and thy house."*

A. The *Hearing* of God's Word

It has already been established that every lost soul in need of salvation must first of all hear the Word of God before salvation can take place. Since this is a certainty, it is imperative that we as believers do all we can to plant the seed of the Word in the hearts of all people everywhere. The Bible clarifies further that it is the hearing of the Word that activates one's faith; and faith when applied, is the single most important action that brings joy and pleasure to God. Even the angels in heaven rejoice at the salvation of one soul. Your faith in God will provoke His continued presence and workings in your life.

In Romans 10:17, we are reminded that since faith cometh by hearing, and hearing by the Word of God, saving faith occurs when a man/woman from God's throne (a believer) brings a Word that is centered in the Person and work of Jesus Christ, the Savior.

Salvation, then, can come in none other name or creed but Jesus Christ through faith in the Word of God. Therefore we must, at all costs, preach Jesus in the totality of His finished work. If you are a preacher reading this book, I urge you to ensure that in your ministration, this should always be your focus (I Corinthians 15:3, 4).

B. To be Saved You Must *believe* God's Word *with all Your Heart*

If one's belief in God's Word does not come from the heart, then that individual's salvation is doubtful. There is a difference between mental faith and heart faith. Mental faith or belief is what one believes only in his/her mind about God. Mental faith says, "I believe in the existence of God," but then there is no heartfelt commitment to the God that you profess to believe in. This kind of faith adds no value to you.

In comparison, heart faith is derived from one's spirit, and embraces every fiber of that individual's being. Heart faith is not stagnant but active.

It is the believer taking action to live for God and to please Him. Without heart faith, there can be no salvation. What then is faith?

1. Faith is the assurance of things hoped for, the evidence of things not seen.
2. Faith means the confidence of what we hope for, the proof of the reality of the things we do not see.

How do I benefit from this Word of God? Study every Scripture on faith or any subject for that matter, meditate upon them, put them into practice, and make God's Word your word.

- If you make God's Word your word, what it produces for the Lord, it will produce for you (Joshua 1:8, Psalms 1:1-3).
- If you make God's Word your word, God's Word will build you into God's reality.
- For God's Word to be very productive in your life, you must continue to keep repeating it to yourself over and over again until it turns into revelation.

The apostle of faith, Smith Wigglesworth said, "There is something about believing God that will cause him to pass over millions of people to get to you." Something that you need to understand is, you cannot substitute faith for love, nor love for faith. Love has her unique place as faith does. Even though they work hand in hand, neither of them can take the place of the other. If you do this you will fail! Everything that we desire to receive from the Lord, we must first of all hope for it.

For example if you need healing, what is the first step you should take? First, you need to hope and believe in God for your healing:

- Hope comes before faith.

- Hope in itself has no substance if it stands alone.
- Faith gives substance to the things hoped for.
- Hope speaks of the future, while faith speaks of the now.
- Hope says tomorrow while faith says today
- Hope says it will come someday while faith says I have it now
- Hope says it will be for me one day, faith says it is mine now.

Where does faith begin? Bible faith begins where the will of God is known. The will of God is the Word of God.

1. Living Word (Jesus Christ) – the Lord Jesus Christ is the living Word of God, our perfect example to follow.
2. The written Word of God – the entire Bible is the will of God for our lives.

In this vein, you can have faith to receive anything and everything that God has promised for you in His Word.

C. Receive and Confess Jesus Christ as Your Lord and Savior

"That if thou shalt confess with thy mouth the Lord Jesus, and shalt believe in thine heart that God hath raised Him from the dead, thou shalt be saved. For with the heart man believeth unto righteousness; and with the mouth confession is made unto salvation" (Romans 10: 9, 10).

The key word in this passage worth studying is the word "confession." Confession here denotes the repetition of the same thing several times. When the LORD said to Moses, "I have given the land of Canaan to Abraham and to his descendants," Israel's responsibility was to keep saying what God had already proclaimed. If Jesus says you are blessed, keep on confessing, "I am blessed."

Rev. Hagin, in his lecture on the Arena of Confessions, stated that you should be very careful about what you say. God locates and justifies you by your confessions. This word has four levels:

1. The Jews' confession of sins (Mark 1:4,5):

    "And there went out unto him (John the Baptist) all the land of Judea, and they of Jerusalem, and were baptized of him in the river of Jordan, confessing their sins (v. 5).

    Observe that this was prior to the coming of the Lord. And the qualification for baptism at the time for the Jews was the confession of their sins. Confessing their sins signified the motives of their hearts, which then became a reality.

2. The confessions of sinners under the New Covenant – these confessions have a major difference from those of the Jews. In the New Testament, the confessions of sinners relate both to confessing their sins, as well as accepting Jesus as Lord and Savior. Jesus took all your sins upon Himself – past, present and future. If He bore the sins of the whole world, then why do you still need to confess your sins? Romans 10:9, 10, remind us that if you confess with your lips that Jesus is Lord and believe in your heart that God raised Him from the dead, then you are saved. These are the only requirements.

The thief on the cross did not have the time to confess all his wickedness before his execution; he only believed and confessed the Lordship of Jesus over his life. He said ***"Lord, remember me when thou comest into thy kingdom"***(Luke 23:42). And instantly the Lord granted his plea.

3. The believer's confession. In this third category, the born again Christian is required to confess his sins every time he misses the mark of righteousness. This confession is for the believer's restoration to fellowship with his Father God, because of his broken relationship with Him, due to his sin. In order to reconnect to God, it is required that the sinning child of God realize his/her mistakes and humbly confess and repent from that sin (I John 1:9).

In the confession of a Jewish national, he received baptism; but in the confession of the Lordship of Jesus Christ by the sinner, he/she receives salvation. When it comes to the confession of our sins as believers, we create the avenue of restoring our broken relationship with the Lord.

4. The fourth dimension of confession is the confession of our faith.

    *   Of God's Word – who we are, what we have and what we can do.
    *   Of Christ our Lord – His Lordship over our lives, our dominion in Him and His work of redemption on our behalf.
    *   Of God our Father – His promises to us, His forgiveness, His love and protection.

The believer's confession of faith and of what he/she believes equals to activated faith. Faith that will definitely move your mountain or your circumstance is your belief plus your confession. In Romans 10:10b, the Word says with your heart belief is born; but with your mouth confession brings into reality that which you have believed in your heart to receive from God.

CHAPTER EIGHT

THE ASSURANCE OF OUR SALVATION

How does one know that he/she is saved? The answer is simple. If you have repented of your sins, have trusted in Christ, and have confessed Him as the Savior and Lord of your life, then you are saved, and the evidence will show.

This is one major revelation that you want to ensure you have experienced. Many religions in the world do not know that one can be saved and be confident of this assurance right here on this earth. Once I had the opportunity to ask a Muslin friend this question: "If you died today, are you sure that the salvation Mohammad gave you can take you to heaven?" His reply was "I don't know; Allah decides when I die."

A similar question was asked of some followers of the Bahai faith about their assurance of salvation and going to heaven when they leave this world. They answered that they were unsure.

The Christian's assurance does not lie in a dead Savior, but in a Savior who resurrected and continues to live in our hearts; a Savior who Himself is the way, the truth and the life; a Savior whose blessed assurance gives us hope that because He lives we, too, can face tomorrow and live eternally with Him in glory; a Savior who continues to fashion our lives for His purpose, glory and praise, in preparation for our heavenly inheritance.

Let me outline some important things that happen when you are truly born again:

A. There is a witness of the Holy Spirit to your spirit that you are a child of God: ***"The Spirit Itself beareth witness with our spirit, that we are the children of God"*** (Romans 8:16). In other words, the Holy Spirit will agree with your own spirit regarding your placement into God's new Holy Family.

B. You will sense the leading of the Holy Spirit in your heart. He will remind you and convict you of sin. The godly nature in you will not give you any joy, peace, or rest when you sin. Instead of sin becoming a pleasure to you, it will be a displeasure: ***"For as many as are led by the Spirit of God, they are the sons of God"*** (Romans 8:14).

As you seek the Holy Spirit's guidance in making every decision in your life, and as you yield your spirit-man to His will and to His way, you will experience His excellent leadership. He makes no mistakes! We have these Words from the wisdom of God in Solomon:

> ***"Trust in the LORD with all thine heart; and lean not unto thine own understanding. In all thy ways acknowledge Him, and He shall direct thy paths"*** (Proverbs 3: 5, 6).

Everything about Christianity has proven to be superior to other religions. But the privilege of having the Lord communicate directly with us can be compared to nothing else. Few years ago when we lived in Tulsa Oklahoma, my wife and I had a serious accident. For her, the result was more serious. Thankfully, she progressed from the stage of not being able to walk alone to walking with clutches. On a Sunday morning during our worship service, I distinctly heard the voice of God saying, "Today your wife will be healed." Secondly he said to me, "Take all the money you brought from home and give it to the man of God." I obeyed the Lord's instruction. After a while, the bishop called for my wife. When he laid his hands upon her and began to pray, she fell under the power of God and was healed instantly. The emphasis here is on the fact that the God of Christians is more than able to lead His sons and daughters, unlike the gods of other religions.

C. The testimony of God's Word – the Bible says whatever God does is forever. This includes the salvation He has offered through His dear Son Jesus Christ. The Word of God also declares that the gifts and calling of God are without repentance. This means, God will never change His mind about the gifts He has given to you, what He has elected you to achieve for Him, and what He will accomplish on your behalf, regardless of past, present, future or unforeseen circumstances – those occurrences in the future that you know nothing about. God has proven to be the immutable or unchangeable God. Let us consider these Scriptures that help us understand our dominion:

"My sheep hear My voice, and I know them, and they follow Me: And I give unto them eternal life; and they shall never perish, neither shall any man pluck them out of My hand. My Father, which gave them Me, is greater than all; and no man is able to pluck them out of my Father's hand. I and my Father are one" (John 10:27-30).

"And this is the record, that God hath given to us eternal life, and this life is in His Son. He that hath the Son hath life; and he that hath not the Son of God hath not life" (1 John 5:11-12).

Does this mean you will not be tried or tempted? Of course not! Adversities are a vital part of our glorious salvation package. As I pointed out earlier, God will see you through these difficult times in your life if you remain with Him. These things are meant for our growth and maturity through faith building. In the end, they reveal our strengths, our weaknesses, as well as our level of growth in the Lord. Paul reminds us that as conquerors in Christ, we are always overcomers. In Romans 8:31, we have another strong assurance: ***"What shall we then say to these things; if God be for us who can be against us?"*** Because of its importance, I'll repeat this question: **Who can be against us**? No one! I declare absolutely no one, by the grace and mercies of our loving heavenly Father! We have the victory over every conflict, trial and temptation; the supply of every need, and the answer to every question. This is because we are safely and securely seated with Christ in heavenly places, far above all principalities and powers.

D. The Manifestation of God's Love in our Hearts

Another witness of the assurance of salvation is the manifestation of God's love in our hearts. Friend, listen to this: it is undisputable that God is love. Since God is love, then we His children are born of His love. As a part of our inheritance, we possess His gene or nature of love. Now, what we need to do is to grow in that love. Hear what God says about love:

> ***"In this the children of God are manifest, and the children of the devil: whosoever doeth not righteousness is not of God, neither he that loveth not his brother. We know that we have passed from death unto life, because we love the brethren. He that loveth not his brother abideth in death"*** (1 John 3: 10, 14).

There are, therefore, three forces that rule the world:

1. Faith – the Bible says if you have faith nothing shall be impossible to you. God can only be moved by faith. So, your faith in God can move on your behalf to do anything for you.

2. Hope – faith is impotent without hope. Hope says there is a future for me tomorrow. Faith says a good one too, and it can be used. Without hope, you cannot live in this world. People who have lost their hope are those who commit suicide. Hope maintains a positive anticipation; it is powerful and will keep you on track no matter the challenges of life.

3. Love – is the greatest of them all. Without love, faith cannot work. Hope can be lost but love cannot fail. Love is powerful because it believes all things, hopes all things and endures all things. The superiority of the force of love over all things is made possible only because love is God Himself.

It is fulfilling to remember that at all times, the primary evidence of our salvation is the manifestation of God's love within us. It should be extended to every aspect of our life in relation to God and man. ***"Beloved, let us love one another: for love is of God; and everyone that loveth is born of God, and knoweth God. He that loveth not knoweth not God; for God is love"*** (I John 4: 7, 8).

E. The Newness of Our Life

One of the results of receiving the new birth is having the newness of life. With the Holy Spirit's replacement of our old life with the new holy life of Christ, the believer is changed forever. It is Christ's presence in your life that is responsible for such a change in your spirit, soul, mind and body: ***"Therefore, if any man be in Christ, he is a new creature, old things are passed away; behold, all things are become new"*** (II Corinthians 5:17). Where and when does this change begin?

1. It begins within your spirit-man.

At salvation when your human spirit is regenerated and you receive God's nature, the life of God permeates your entire spirit and gives it not a reformation, but a spiritual birth. It is God giving birth to your human spirit (John 3:3-7). This is a divine mystery that you will understand only upon experiencing the new birth.

2. It brings about changes in your mind (Romans 12:1, 2)

Your mind, the seat of your intellect and emotions, is transformed by the birth of your human spirit. That is the impartation of the mind of Christ in you. Your new thought process or mindset at this point changes your mentality and approach to life. Whereas you had previously viewed life from a worldly standpoint (love for money, greed, pleasures, immorality), to name a few; your new perspective on life is now changed to that of piety or godliness. This is what Paul says in I Corinthians 2:16:

> *"For who hath known the mind of the Lord, that he may instruct Him? But we have the mind of Christ."*

We have read that Solomon's wisdom surpassed that of all the wise men of his day, but believers have within them the One whose wisdom is most extensive and infinite. His name is Jesus, the Son of the living God! To have Christ living within us is to have access to the mind of Christ. In the book of Daniel chapter one, Daniel, Shadrach, Meshach and Abenego were blessed with exceeding wisdom, beyond that of all the wise men of Great Babylon: magicians, sorcerers and astrologers.

A greater then these four brilliant young men resides in you and me, Hallelujah! From this day forward, I urge you to think and behave as children of God that possess His wisdom. Our days of defeat are over! We have all it takes to properly utilize the gifts the Lord has apportioned to us. We are equipped to conquer the world for Jesus.

[Prayer]: *I prophesy that in the name of Jesus, the supernatural capability of the creative mind of Christ enters you now. That from today onward, your mind will never be the same, and that you will use your mind to honor and serve the Lord, in Jesus' mighty name, AMEN!*

2. Your body takes on a *new* "form"

Even your body changes when Jesus Christ takes over your life. Let me share my own personal experience with you. All the demons of sicknesses, diseases and death fled when the One that holds true ownership to my body entered in me. With great joy, I now testify that my body has rested from drinking, smoking, and fighting. Presently, I experience soundness and vitality in my body, soul and spirit. From the inception of the Lord's coming into my life, my real youthfulness began. I believe that as a result of the misuse of their bodies, some people have actually shortened their life span, and many have passed on before their proper time.

God wants us to live in absolute prosperity on the earth. But this can only be accomplished if we fully present our bodies as a living temple for the Lord, because they no longer belong to us. Please read I Corinthians 3:16, 17; 6:19, 20.

C. There is an evidence of the fruit of your regenerated spirit. Where the indwelling presence of the Holy Spirit truly abides in a believer, the evidence will clearly be demonstrated in the fruits he/she bears:

"But the fruit of the Spirit is love, joy, peace, longsuffering, gentleness, goodness, faith, Meekness, temperance: against such there is no law. And they that are Christ's have crucified the flesh with the affections and lusts" (Galatians 5:22-24).

Do you know that the "fruit of the Spirit" are evidences of your regeneration? In actuality, this is the result of the Spirit of God completely taking control of your life and manifesting His presence in the totality of Christian living. Your regenerated spirit is your new nature – the nature of Christ which has taken residence in you to rule over your spirit, soul and body. Christ's justification is a solid attestation of how God considers your life in His. To Him, you are special and loved; someone to whom He has freely accorded all the benefits of the new birth.

Recognizing that you did nothing to gain these benefits but to believe on Him should be a very grateful and humbling experience. The nature of God in you will bring you to a place of absolute obedience and surrender. These virtues are expressions of your implicit faith and confidence in the Lord. They will allow you to appropriate all His promises to your life, as His Holy Spirit works in you, internally and externally, cultivating you into becoming a vessel of honor. By His Spirit, the Lord is then able to manifest in your life through the fruit of love, joy, peace, longsuffering, gentleness, goodness, faith, meekness, and temperance. At this maturity level, you are a replica of what you claim to be, and whom you profess to represent – a faithful and obedient Christian; a follower of Jesus Christ, the Son of God who emptied Himself and was made in the likeness of men (Philippians 2:5-11). You must, therefore, willingly surrender all you are to the Lord so that He can freely do with you what pleases Him. I want to assure you that if all of the "fruit of the Spirit" are not yet bearing in your life, do not give up! Only remain steadfast in and yielded to the Lord, so that His Holy Spirit can process you for the benefit of the hurting people of the world. They need you in order to come to the Master.

CHAPTER NINE

THE RESULTS AND BENEFITS OF OUR SALVATION

There are no significant benefits in the world today than the benefits the children of God receive when they are birthed into God's Family. As sons and daughters, we are inheritors to the throne of God through our Lord Jesus Christ. Everything the Father owns belongs to us.

Mention has already been made of some of these benefits, but for emphasis purposes, I would love for us to discuss a few in the order we have received them:

A. Our Spiritual Benefits

1. We become possessors of God's eternal life. Eternal life does not just mean life without end. It also means that we, having become partakers of the very nature of the Holy One, have His life.

God being supernatural, His divine nature gives us His supernatural life. Our life of superiority instantly takes us out of the life of the ordinary, spiritually and physically, into the eternal presence of God. Jesus answered them, ***"… Is it not written in your law, I said, Ye are gods? If He called*** *them gods, unto whom the word of God came and the scripture cannot be broken; Say ye of Him, whom the Father hath sanctified, and sent into the world, Thou blasphemest; because I said, I am the Son of God?"* (John 10:34-36).

I agree that in no way could the Scriptures ever be broken. If He calls us His little "gods" on the earth, who can dispute this declaration? Who or what can stand against His Word? Oh! How much I look forward to you being enlightened, and this truth sinking into your heart (Ephesians 1:17-23). Why not open up your spirit, your soul and your mind so that you can rise above defeat and experience victory in Jesus?

[Prayer]: *I take authority in the name of Jesus and command your mind to be opened to God's class of life, Amen!*

2. I Peter 2:9 clearly states how God sees you relative to your new level or class of royalty on the earth. It is a direct connection and relationship to the King of Kings and the Lord of Lords. This status awards you with a rating so high, you can no longer afford to live comfortably in the "pigpen" of filth – like the old sinner you once were. As a chosen one and an integral part of the Family of God, you are destined for greatness, honor, integrity and Godly leadership.

Daniel and his three friends fully understood this fact; they recognized their royal status. Holding fast to this revelation, they were able to boldly stand up against God's enemies in Babylon. Even in that strange heathen land, they ruled and reigned; they influenced profound changes to the decrees of kings; they shut the mouths of starving lions, and they survived the hottest blazing fiery furnace, which proved to be as cool as air to them. Let us just say in simple terms, you and I are **God's special representatives** on the earth.

3. Our spiritual dominion is restored unto us

I have explained this fact from the onset of writing this book. Due to its essence, I want to again state that the dominion Adam, the first son of God lost to his enemy in the Garden, has been regained at Calvary for us. We are reminded of the declarations of the Lord in following passages:

"… All power is given unto Me in heaven and in earth. Go ye therefore…" (Matthew 28:18, 19).

4. The believing one is now the home of the Holy of Hollies of God, as it was in the Old Testament. Here is what God says about you and me as His Holy of Holies:

"Know ye not that ye are the temple of God, and that the Spirit of God dwelleth in you? If any man defile the temple of God, him shall God destroy; for the temple of God is holy, which temple ye are" (I Corinthians 3:16, 17).

Our restored abilities, empowerment and authority to rule and reign on the earth can only be accomplished through Christ Jesus who is the Author and the Leader of our salvation. Therefore child of God, I encourage you to rise up to your rightful position of authority and power.

What a mystery that the God who made the heavens and the earth dwells within us. He is the God that Mount Sinai could not withstand when He descended upon it. He is the same God whose glorious presence the children of Israel could not bear even from a far distance.

The blessed realization that the Holy God of heaven has made His abode in us should be more than sufficient reason why we believers should live in and pursue holiness all the days of our lives. Holiness enables us to maintain the activated presence of the Holy Spirit. Only then can our worship and service be acceptable to God and blessed by Him; only then can we live victoriously over Satan. We are to be reminded that the Bible describes this ferocious enemy as a roaring lion, seeking whom he may devour. Be on your watch!

> *"What? Know ye not that your body is the temple of the Holy Ghost which is in you, which ye have of God, and ye are not your own? For you are bought with a price: therefore glorify God in your body, and in your spirit, which are God's"*(I Corinthians 6:19, 20).

[Prayer]: *Lord, please let these mighty Holy Ghost oriented Words of God be conceived in our spirits, in Jesus' name, Amen!*

If we fail to become impregnated with these Words, the presence of God in us will never be revealed. Instead, it is the sinful nature, still craftily laying in wait that will manifest in us as disobedience and opposition to God. I pray that as the Lord has already began to work in you, you will yield to the Spirit in seeing yourself as the one whose holy life should resemble that of the Lord's on the earth. Let us see what II Corinthians 6:16 says:

> *"...for ye are the temple of the living God; as God hath said, I will dwell in them, and walk in them; and I will be their God, and they shall be My people."*

5. You and I now have access to God's presence at all times. Being in His presence also gives us the privilege of approaching the throne of God. The Law stood as a barrier to the Old Testament saints accomplishing this. Before Christ shed His precious blood, the Law was man's school master and sin his slave master. It is an honor to be in God's company.

A good lesson to remember is that the company to which you belong could very well determine your success or failure. The Lord has promised that He will be with us until the end of the world (Matthew 28:20). What a pleasant reassurance that our hopes and expectations in the Lord will always abide, never to be cut off, because we are His righteousness. Satan knows believers have a bright future, so he puts up a grand struggle to pull us on his side. He aims at robbing us of our access to the presence of God. But thanks be unto Him who has given us the power to overcome all the devices of the enemy. In His presence they are powerless.

[Prayer]: *Child of God stay in God's presence and rest. It is in His presence that you have a glorious future.*

6. You and I now have access to God's voice forever: ***"My sheep hear My voice, and I know them, and they follow Me"*** (John 10:27). The remarkable opportunity to hear the voice of God is of extreme importance and necessity to your success in life. Every triumph begins with you hearing the voice of the Lord. As you pray, you must always learn to listen for, recognize, and obey God's voice. If you operate within these boundaries, there will not be any room for errors in your life because:

    • Your faith becomes foolishness when you have not heard from God, but act on your own accord.
    • If God does not command or approve, you have no guarantee for His backing.
    • Everyone who is making or has made genuine advancements in the kingdom of God first heard from Him.

We have been blessed because of the obedience of Archbishop Joel and Mama Loretta Laurore, in recognizing and obeying the clear voice of God.

As a result, the World Revival Temple Ministry was established in Tulsa, Oklahoma, some 30 years ago. The ministry is touching the earth with God's message and power. ***God's success is overtaking them because they obeyed His marching orders.*** Let us all do likewise as sons and daughters of God. Our key is the mighty voice of God.

7. You and I now have guaranteed protection in the Lord. The Bible says to us in Ephesians 4:26, 27: ***"Be angry and sin not: let not the sun go down upon your wrath: neither give place to the devil."*** The devil has no access to our lives unless we permit him. Satan could only take Adam's place upon Adam's personal permission. Similarly, Judas Iscariot willingly gave Satan his place and Satan destroyed him. King Saul did likewise, and the enemy robbed him of his dignity and his crown.

Our Lord Jesus Christ was the only exception. When Satan attempted to take his place, he (Satan) failed miserably. For the Lord could never have allowed Satan to rule over Him. Friend, hear what God says about your security in Christ, according to Psalm 91:1: ***"He that dwelleth in the secret place of the Most High shall abide under the shadow of the Almighty."*** What is that secret place? It is abiding in Christ! As a matter of fact, the whole of Psalm 91 is based on your guaranteed security. Read it and meditate upon it. The protection that we have in God is forever! (Psalm 125: 1-2).

Do you have faith in God? If you do, then trust in Him all the way; trust Him with your whole heart; trust Him to see you through, no matter what adversity may come your way. The enemy's intention was for Job to blaspheme God. He's making the same assertions about you:

> ***"Then Satan answered the LORD, and said, Doth Job fear God for naught? Hast not thou made a hedge about him, and about***

139

his house, and about all that he hath on every side? Thou hast blessed the work of his hands, and his substance is increased in the land" (Job 1: 9, 10).

[Prayer]: *Satan I rebuke you in the name of Jesus because our God will not withdraw His covering from us, Amen!*

"But put forth Thine hand now, and touch all that he hath, and he will curse Thee to Thy face" (Job 1:11).

Job did not curse God. His faith is an excellent example of that which is characterized by patience and persistence (James 5:11). Like Job, even when we are faced with trials and temptations, the Lord controls the limit of the enemy, depending on our spiritual strength in Him (Job 1:12). Gloriously, part of the guarantee of our security is that every child of God is the ***apple of His eye.*** You do not need to fear; the Lord is on your side.

B. Our Physical Benefits

Some of the essential physical benefits we enjoy as sons and daughters of God are:

1. The restoration of our bodies to health: ***"Beloved, I wish above all things that thou mayest prosper and be in health, even as thy soul prospereth"*** (III John 2).

We are aware that our prosperity in health is a priority among the physical benefits we enjoy as sons and daughters of God. Maintaining a healthy status in life is one of the major factors that determines whether or not a believer is enjoying the best quality of life. This state of wellbeing has been provided only by our Lord Jesus Christ.

And so, God's total health package for mankind was a vital component of His overall redemptive plan to restore us back to Himself after the First Adam sinned (Isaiah 53:4, 5). Even in the Old Testament, we have seen how God delivered His people from sicknesses and diseases; these curses were not meant to be a part of the lives of the Israelites(Exodus 15:26). Look at Deuteronomy 7:15:

> *"And the LORD will take away from thee all sickness, and will put none of the evil diseases of Egypt, which thou knowest, upon thee; but will lay them upon all them that hate thee."*

As long as you abide in Christ and His love, then the "sicknesses and diseases of Egypt," (as a type of the world today), will not overtake you. You must forever acknowledge that Christ's atonement covered every curse for you.

2. The restoration of our longevity on planet earth. Have you ever thought about living long on the earth? Do you know that God who made us and has saved us wants us to live and fulfill all our God-ordained years and dreams on this earth? Yes, this is God's perfect plan for you and me. Whatever God has promised us, it is our privilege to enjoy, in Christ Jesus.

Beloved, long life in excellent health is God's best plan for you and me. Take a look at Deuteronomy 11:21:

> *"That your days may be multiplied, and the days of your children, in the land which the LORD sware unto your fathers to give them, as the days of heaven upon the earth."*

All our covenant fathers including Abraham, Isaac, and Jacob lived very long. Abraham lived for 175 years, Isaac 180 years, and Jacob 147 years. Moses the man of God lived for 120 years. His eyes were not even dimmed, neither did he lose his natural vitality. Caleb, at the age of 80, was so strong that he led Israel in various battles against their enemies. He took his God-given heritage and was victorious. I have cited these examples to remind you that what God accomplished in the Old Covenant He can still do today, because the New Covenant is built on better promises. In I Chronicles 29:28 we read this about the life of David: ***"And he died in a good old age, full of days, riches, and honor…"*** Beloved, is this not what you desire? I do!

C. Our Material Benefits

Included in our total redemptive benefit package is also our material benefit. This is another demonstration of God's love for His own, and His concern for our overall wholesomeness.

Like Moses, you will notice that even though the patriarchs did not live under the New Covenant Dispensation, yet the LORD did not withhold any blessing from them. They were not only blessed with long life, they also had an abundance of all the other blessings. Isaac, for example, was so rich that the Philistines envied him (Genesis 26:12-14).

> ***"And Abraham was old, and well stricken in age: and the LORD had blessed Abraham in all things" (24: 1).***

Turning to the early Church in the New Testament, the saints of God prospered so much that there wasn't any lack among them (Acts 4:33-37). The Apostle Paul assures us that our God is faithful and shall supply all our needs according to His riches in glory by Christ Jesus. If the Lord gave His very life for us, surely He, together with His Father, can give us all things.

In II Corinthians 8:9, the Word of God reveals that the incomparable grace of God enabled Christ to basically abandon His riches in heaven for your sake and became poor, so that through His poverty you could become rich.

Indeed, the undeserved grace of Jesus Christ our Redeemer upon our lives has translated us from physical, spiritual, and material poverty into His marvelous light and glorious riches.

CHAPTER TEN

SALVATION IN TENSES

From the judicial system of law in heaven, there are three levels of righteousness. They can also be classified as the three tenses of salvation.

In the context of this discussion, righteousness means to have a right standing with God. There is a difference between the righteousness of God and that of man. Biblical righteousness is defined as:

1. The standards that the holy God has set in place to govern His universe.
2. God's voice proclaimed upon anything, any being, or any government.
3. Doing the will of God wholeheartedly.
4. Taking God at His Word.

Salvation has three stages, as it relates to believers:

A. The PAST TENSE of Salvation

The past tense of salvation is the emphatic declaration that you have been saved from the guilt and penalty of sin. Since you have accepted Christ Jesus as your Savior and Lord, you are freed from the guilt and penalty of sin that is upon unbelievers. This is explained in Romans 8:1-2:

"There is therefore now no condemnation to them which are in Christ Jesus, who walk not after the flesh, but after the Spirit. For the law of the Spirit of life in Christ Jesus hath made me free from the law of sin and death."

Now, the question that obviously comes to mind relates to what and who is responsible for the removal of the guilt and penalty of your sins. Without a doubt, you are already aware that it is the death of Christ Jesus, the Messiah. *"For He hath made Him (Christ) to be sin for us, who knew no sin; that we might be made the righteousness of God in Him."*

Therefore, because you have made Jesus Christ your Lord and Savior, you are freed from God's righteous judgment. You have now passed from death to life according to John 5:24:

"Verily, verily, I say unto you, He that heareth My word, and believeth on Him that sent Me, hath everlasting life, and shall not come into condemnation; but is passed from death unto life."

This infers that you have been justified or made righteous through Christ, on the basis of His righteousness. Once justified, your sanctification occurred at the moment you received Christ. You have been separated from sin and set apart unto God by the same act that justified you.

To explain this further, the past tense of salvation has to do with your initial righteousness. In II Corinthians 5:21 the Word says that God made Christ who knew no sin to be sin for us, that we might be made the righteousness of God in Him. Please understand this: that we have been made the righteousness of God *only* in Him. You did not make yourself righteous, but you were made righteous.

145

B. The PRESENT TENSE of Salvation

This is what I call progressive righteousness – you are being saved from the power of sin. This aspect of salvation has to do with your power over sin. Daily you experience victory over sin. The holy nature of God living within you allows you to practice progressive sanctification. You do this by yielding yourself and everything that you are to the Lord, and by crucifying your flesh. Thus, God's Holy Spirit enables you to have dominion over sin (Romans 6:12-14):

> *"Let not sin therefore reign in your mortal body, that ye should obey it in the lusts thereof. Neither yield ye your members as instruments of unrighteousness unto sin: but yield yourselves unto God, as those that are alive from the dead, and your members as instruments of righteousness unto God. For sin shall not have dominion over you: for ye are not under the law, but under grace."*

In the past tense of salvation, progressive righteousness is a must. The word progressive means to advance, to go forward, or to make headways. This level requires that you:

1. Work out your own salvation, in becoming like Christ your Lord.
2. Develop your Christian character in the school of the spirit.
3. Disagree to do wrong, but agree to do right.
4. Grow from the stage of a baby Christian to that of a matured believer.

Paul the apostle said of himself, when he was a child he spoke as a child, he understood as a child, he thought as a child; but when he became a man, he put away childish things (I Corinthians 13:11).

C. The FUTURE TENSE of Salvation

The future tense of salvation has to do with the believer being delivered completely from the presence of sin. There will come a time when all believers will be taken away from the presence of evil. It will also be the time when evil will be completely taken away from the midst of believers – when Christ returns and takes His Church to heaven.

In heaven, evil does not exist. The New Jerusalem, the Holy City of God, will also be freed of sin. I John 3:2, 3 cite these Words:

> *"Beloved, now are we the sons of God, and it doth not yet appear what we shall be: but we know that, when he shall appear, we shall be like Him; for we shall see Him as He is. And every man that hath this hope in Him purified himself, even as He is pure."*

My friend, this is truly wonderful and exciting news for us! We await the day of Jesus' coming, when we will be with Him forever and ever in glory, Amen!

CHAPTER ELEVEN

HOW DOES ONE EXPERIENCE MATURITY IN SALVATION?

A. A Daily *Study of God's Word*

As food is necessary for the nourishment and growth of our human bodies, so also and more indispensable is the Word of God to our spirits. In Joshua 1:8 we are told to study the Word:

> *"This book of the law shall not depart out of thy mouth; but thou shalt meditate therein day and night, that thou mayest observe to do according to all that is written therein: for then thou shalt make thy way prosperous, and then thou shalt have good success."*

It is your intake of God's Word that determines your output of Christian virtues, in terms of applying godly standards in all your efforts and undertakings. Your personal growth as a Christian steward requires consistency in studying and meditating on the Word. This is a call to discipline, diligence and commitment. By so doing and with the help of the Spirit, the believer is then better equipped to apply the Word to his/her life. Knowledge is power!

It is not at all coincidental that the very first Psalm in the book of Psalms speaks about the longevity and fruitfulness that is destined for the one that lives for God and delights in His Word:

> *"Blessed is the man that walketh not in the counsel of the ungodly, nor standeth in the way of sinners, nor sitteth in the seat of the scornful. But his delight is in the law of the LORD; and in His law doth he meditate day and night. And he shall be like a tree planted by the rivers of water, that bringeth forth its fruit in its season; its leaf also shall not wither; and whatsoever he doeth shall prosper" (Psalms 1:1-3).*

Do you want to prosper in your walk with the Lord? Do you want to please Him? If your answer is yes, do as He has said. In II Timothy 2:15 we are commanded to study so as to show ourselves approved unto God and to unashamedly and rightly divide the Word of truth. Paul called upon believers to desire the sincere milk of the Word that we may grow thereby.

Here are some wisdom nuggets that I want to share with you:

1. It is the treatment you give to God's Word that will determine your height in life.
2. Until God's Word becomes your word of life, you have no guaranteed future.
3. It is your obedience to God's Word that reduces your enemies to nothing.
4. When you obey God's Word at His command, God will establish His Word at the time of your need.

5. Until you align your life with God's Word, the Word will not work for you.

6. Every Word of God you obey puts you up and every Word of God you despise brings you down.

7. Your success in life will therefore be the product of your obedience to God's Word. Who so despiseth the Word shall be destroyed: But he that feareth the commandment shall be rewarded, says the wisdom of Solomon.

What is in God's Word that makes it the most popular book, the most read, the most accurate, and the most alive book in the world today?

1. The Bible contains God's power. In Romans 1:16 Paul said he was not ashamed of the Gospel of Christ, for it is the power of God unto salvation to everyone that believes.

God's Word is the most prominent agent of human salvation in all spheres of life. It carries healing power, deliverance power, and transforming power. Master Jesus said His Words are Spirit and life. The Word has a supernatural quickening power that makes our human spirits alive. Study God's Word, meditate upon it, love it and use it to make your life colorful and attractive on the earth.

2. The Bible carries the very life of God (John 6:63). Every Word of God is loaded with divine nature. The more of God's Word you impart into your spirit, the more you become like Jesus, and the better you live on the earth.

3. The Word of God is the divine carrier of health – make it your daily meal. It is said of Wigglesworth that he never allowed himself to go about thirty minutes without reading his Bible. He ate the Word and the Word manifested through him in signs and wonders. In Proverbs

4:22, we are told the Word is life unto those that find it, and health to all their flesh. The Bible is God's prescription for our human flesh. It heals our bodies.

4. God's Word is the solution to every problem of life:

    a. It is the solution to our sin problem. It gives us the way out of sin, and it cleanses us from all unrighteousness. It provides the ground for repentance, confession, redemption, forgiveness and reconciliation (Isaiah 1:18, 19).

    b. God's Word is the solution to all our poverty problems. If you believe God's Word and obey it, it can take you out of poverty. The Bible way is the best way to prosper on the earth. Proverbs10:22 says the blessings of the Lord maketh rich and He addeth no sorrows. When God prospers you, along with that prosperity, He gives you peace, joy, security and satisfaction. Worldly prosperity lacks all of these blessings.

Consequently, from God's perspective, you will prosper through the knowledge of His Word. Set your heart on studying the Bible for your own discovery. Make up your mind to obey every Word of God that crosses your path.

If you want the nations of the earth to locate you, obey the Word of God. If you have the desire to make an impact upon your generation, follow God's Word. Are you interested in growing your business? Obey Scriptural principles. Love God, live clean, serve others, live in peace with all men as much as lies within you, and pay your tithes and offerings to your local Church.

5. God's Word is the answer to all impossible problems (Genesis 18:9-14). There are problems on the earth that you cannot solve alone; neither

can your parents, your doctor, your president nor even your pastor. Whenever you are confronted with such problems, remember that God's Word cannot fail. You know the story of Ma Sarah and Father Abraham. They lived all their lives up to a century without a child. But when the Word of the Lord came unto them, everything about them changed. Their natural bodies were revitalized and accelerated. Their strengths and desires were also rehabilitated. Because of the spoken Word of God, Ma Sarah conceived and brought forth her first child since marriage. After that, she lived thirty-seven more years and Abraham lived seventy-five additional years, remarried and bore more sons and daughters.

B. The Child of God Must Develop *a Daily Life of Prayer*

1. Prayer is pouring out your heart to God.
2. Prayer is God's heart beating in yours.
3. It is a spiritual dialog between the daddy and the son/daughter.

Why is prayer important?

1. Prayer is very important in the life of every believer because it is the means by which we breathe out to God spiritually. It is the breath of your human spirit. If your inner man will live healthily, it must continue to breathe. Just as your physical body cannot survive without your physical breath, so also your inward man cannot live without breathing.
2. Prayer is important because it is the means by which we give God Almighty permission to act on our behalf on the earth. In Mark 10:46-52 – Blind Bartimaeus was visually impaired for many years. Jesus the healer was in his city, but did not observe his presence until he cried out for help. And as he did, Jesus responded immediately.

King Hezekiah was sick to death. The Prophet Isaiah was sent by the LORD to inform him to put his house in order, for his death was eminent. Hezekiah took action by heightening his faith – he turned his face towards the wall and prayed with humility and urgency. God heard him, healed him and gave him fifteen more years to live. His prayer ultimately changed his situation (Isaiah 38:1-5).

3. Prayer is vital because it helps believers to overcome temptations and trials. Jesus urges us to watch and pray that we enter not into temptation; not giving in to the weaknesses of the flesh, but relying on the willingness and power of the Spirit to always strengthen us. Even Christ the Son of God needed the strength of His dear Father in His hour of humiliation and suffering.

When you learn to pray fervently and constantly, you will escape the many temptations of the enemy. Prayer is your most effective weapon and your asset in gaining kingdom power and making your life fruitful. You are the key to your own success. Remember this: a Christian who is not prayerful is a powerless Christian.

The "dialing tone" of prayer

Are you aware that God wants to answer your prayer whenever you call upon Him? Your "dialing tone" to prayer prepares your spirit, soul and body to be able to provoke the keen attention of the Lord:

a. Know God's promises for your situation – you must ask yourself if there are any Scriptural promises for you in the Word of God. Jeremiah 33:3 gives you the right to call upon heaven when you have a problem. Before you start praying, remind God of His promises to you; then stand upon His promised Word and call upon Him to help you. Psalm 50:15 is another promise from God if you find yourself in trouble. He directs you to call upon Him in the day of trouble and He will deliver you. Are you in trouble? Use this Scripture to get out by calling unto God your Father.

b. Pray without any habitual sin in your life. God will always love you, but He never compromises with sin. David's realization of this significant truth led him to remind himself against holding iniquity in his heart, so that he could not prevent the Lord from hearing his prayer. In Isaiah 59:1 the prophet said, the hand of the LORD is not shortened that it cannot save; neither is His ear heavy that it cannot hear, but our iniquities have separated us from Him. Thus when you pray, confess your sins, forsake them and forgive those that have wronged you.

c. Doubts and unbelief versus faith. Your unbelief and doubts result into wasted prayers. The Word of God says, he that cometh to God must believe that He is, and He rewards those that diligently seek Him (Matthew 17:20; Hebrews 11:6). Without faith, you cannot obtain anything from God. He is the God of faith, and you must be a child of faith to receive from Him (Mark11:22-24).

Where do you begin?

1. Begin with thanksgiving unto God for whatever He has done for you (Psalm 103:1).
2. Learn to worship the Lord in your own closet or at your altar. (Worship means to say to God how much He is worth, how great and powerful He is, and how lovely and wonderful He is and has been to you).
3. Talk to Him as your Father; discuss issues of your heart; tell Him about your happiness, your downfalls, and your desires.
4. Talk to Him about your family and friends.

5. Learn to listen to Him also; He will speak to you. Be quiet before Him and listen to your spirit-man (Acts 13:1, 2).

C. Learn to *Fellowship With Other Believers*

Paul in Hebrews 10:25 warns believers not to forsake the assembling of ourselves together, meaning that we should never abandon gathering together on a regular basis. As sons and daughters of God, this should be a bounding duty and joy, but it requires a conscious effort and personal commitment. We congregate primarily to study God's Word, to worship and praise Him, to intercede for ourselves and others, to evangelize the lost and to carry out various other Christian duties within the Church, our communities and the larger world.

Believers are closely knitted, with a dependency on one another, much like lighted coals that need a close bond if they are to maintain heat and life: once scattered, they lose the ability to remain alive. Through the expression of mutual love and care for one another, by our presence, fellowship, strength and encouragement, we maintain a relationship that speaks of the lovable presence of the Lord in our lives. His presence boosts our ability to continuously exhibit a prioritized dedication to His mission and calling.

Our fellowship as brothers and sisters in Christ is so vital that we cannot possibly survive spiritually or physically without it. We rely upon one another to the effect that we must each serve as a reciprocator of good will. This plays a crucial role in our overall Christian growth. Let us remember the instruction the Lord gave to His disciples before His departure from this earth: that they should love one another, for it is only by so doing that the world would know that they were His disciples.

As a child of God, you must consciously decide to create healthy relationships, while developing Christian character. This depends on the company or relationships you keep, and how you separate yourself from the unbelieving friends you had before you gave your life to

Christ. They are a huge hindrance to your growth in the Lord: *"He that walketh with wise men shall be wise: but a companion of fools shall be destroyed"*.

When you consider just whom you are in Christ, your disconnection from these people matters very much. If you continue to associate with them, they may influence you to return to your old ways. Matthew 7:6 speaks of two groups of people that we are to disassociate ourselves from:

1. The unstable Christians who go back to their vomits;
2. The sinners who are rolling in sin.

> *"Give not that which is holy unto the dogs, neither cast ye your pearls before swine, lest they trample them under their feet, and turn again and rend you."*

Here, dogs are considered to be the unstable Christians that return to their vomits, as dogs do. The swine typify sinners that have no fear of God and are living like pigs. Again, God's Word says:

> *"Wherefore come out from among them, and be ye separate, saith the Lord, and touch not the unclean thing; and I will receive you, And will be a Father unto you, and ye shall be My sons and daughters, saith the Lord Almighty" (II Corinthians 6:17-18).*

D. Share your new faith with others:

And Jesus came and spake unto them saying, *"… All power is given unto me in heaven and in earth. Go ye therefore, and teach all nations, baptizing them in the name of the Father, and of the Son, and of the Holy Ghost: Teaching them to observe all things whatsoever I have commanded you: and, lo, I am with you always, even unto the end of the world. Amen"* *(Matthew 28: 18-20).*

This is the command from our great Captain, the LORD JESUS. Do not be ashamed to witness to people, especially to your relatives and friends about your glorious experience in Christ. To begin with, there are three aspects of your life that you really need to share:

1. Your Life **Before** Christ

For example, when I was not a Christian, I lived to please myself. I did many terrible things such as my intention to fight my father – the reason being, I felt that his actions at that particular time were wrong. Moreover, I was very disobedient to my parents; I stole and lied on many occasions. Other details of my pre-Christian life are explained throughout this book.

2. Your **Encounter with Jesus**.

The day on which you accepted Jesus Christ as your Savior and Lord was your day of encounter with Him. You now need to share how God saved you and transformed your life. Focus on the positive changes you have experienced since you became a Christian.

3. Share your **Victories and Failures**

Sharing your victories and failures since you began to walk with the Lord is very helpful to others in their own Christian walk with the Lord.

Below are other examples of my personal encounters during my earlier walk with the Lord while in Liberia:

a.   My faith in Christ was tested many times:

One morning, a heated disagreement between my brother and me over his bad, defiant attitude eventually led to a bitter physical fight. The most important aspect of this story is that, the fighting smeared my Christian testimony in the community. I, however, repented and asked the Lord to forgive me, and He did.

b.   At another time, I started a serious confrontation with a local police officer, for his refusal to repay an outstanding indebtedness to me. Not only was the officer unapologetic, he also spat in my face. Prior to that time, his actions would have caused an instant outrage and aggressive retaliation on my part. But thanks be to God, I heeded to the voice of the Holy Spirit to hold my peace and walk away. Unlike the former experience with my brother, I did not yield to the temptation to react in ways that would have damaged my Christian integrity and caused me to dishonor the name of the Lord.

Friend, each time temptations come your way and you can yield to the Spirit's direction in overcoming them, you have won another victory over the enemy. If not, you will continue to be entrapped and used by Satan. I sincerely trust that these testimonies will encourage you. Do not be afraid to share your victories and failures.

E. Learn to Forgive Yourself of the Past

Do not allow your past sins to hunt or hold you down. Be mindful that when God forgives you, He remembers your sins no more – they have been washed by the blood of Jesus Christ. And whatever the blood of Jesus washes can never be found again:

> *"...For as the heaven is high above the earth, so great is His mercy toward them that fear Him. As far as the east is from the west, so far hath He removed our transgressions from us"* (Psalm 103:10-12).

F. Be Quick to Forgive Others When They do You Wrong:

Christ showed believers the example of forgiveness when He, through His humiliation and sufferings at Calvary forgave our sins, even though we were still sinners. His call for us to practice forgiveness is borne out of His amazing grace and love for us. In the prayer model He taught His disciples, believers are to seek to be forgiven of their sins, even as they forgive those who sin against them (Matthew 6:12). But Christ warned in verse 15 that if believers do not forgive, neither will God forgive them. This teaching is simple and practical: that you should do unto others as you would have them do unto you; more so, as it relates to being forgiven of the Lord and receiving His blessings in its fullness.

In Matthew 5:44, the Lord even commands believers to love their enemies, to bless those that curse them, to do good to those that hate them, and to pray for those that despitefully use and persecute them. They are to turn the other cheek instead of retaliating. This is far different from the dictates of the Law under that Dispensation. It demanded an eye for an eye and a tooth for a tooth.

The liberty, mercy, compassion, divine favor, forgiveness and grace exhibited under the New Covenant are just so marvelous. They completely oppose those of the Old Testament in which punishment for sins was meted out within the full context of the Law, with a flare of vengeance and harshness. In John 8:1-11, we read about the story of the woman caught in the immoral act of adultery. The Judaizes, who did not believe in Christ and His teachings, were about to apply the Law by stoning her to death, but by the timely intervention of Christ, her life was spared. To say the least, both she and her accusers were taken aback by the Lord's show of mercy – the kind only He has brought to the world because He came to take away sins and bring men back to God.

The New Testament teachings were difficult to be understood, even by the disciples of Jesus Christ. In Matthew 18:21-22, Peter tried to understand the doctrine of forgiveness. He asked Jesus how often was he to extend forgiveness to his brother for offenses against him. Peter was justified in asking this question because in his human mind, he thought he was allowed to forgive his brother only seven times. What a disaster! But the master indicated to him that it would actually take seventy times seven or 490 times. In Ephesians 4:26, remember that Paul advised believers not to allow the sun to go down on their anger? This is to say that in context, Jesus' response to Peter applied to only a day. In short, believers should decide to forgive like Christ does – swiftly and selflessly.

Remember that tolerance, patience and endurance are not weaknesses, but spiritual strengths and virtues that go a long way in keeping the unity of the faith among believers. Paul reminds us that we function under one Lord, one faith, and one baptism. In any conflict of life, be it between a couple, a friend, a business partner or Christian brethren, the most matured person is the one who has the heart to truly forgive and move on. He/she does not always insist on "rightness," but is willing and ready to leave room for reconciliation and for the power of God to work. Retaining grudges and unforgiveness is a result of the manipulation of the enemy. You are no more under His dominion. Do not permit him to destroy your life and prolong the conflict and disunity within the Body of Christ.

G. What Happens When You Fall into Sin?

Whenever you walk in disobedience to the Lord, rise up quickly and keep moving with Jesus (I John 1: 9). Do not forget the willingness and faithfulness of God to forgive all confessed and repented sins, and cleanse you from all unrighteousness. Holiness is the primary characteristic of a Christian. You must be determined to serve the Lord in purity. I Peter 1:13-16 commands us to be holy, as He who has called us is holy – in all manner of conversation.

Let us examine the story of David. When he sinned against God and the people of Israel by committing adultery and murder, the LORD God forgave him upon his true repentance (Psalms 51:1-12). David fully acknowledged his transgressions and pled for mercy from a loving and kind God; The God whose compassion is renewed morning after morning, causing us to receive new mercies on a daily basis.

David did not only receive the LORD's forgiveness, he was also restored to the throne of Israel. God remembered his sins no more. He allowed him to marry Bathsheba, following the death of her husband Uriah. This was the very woman with whom David had committed adultery. Earlier on, David had carefully planned and executed Uriah's death to cover up his sin with Bathsheba. Then, in God's providence, David and Bathsheba had a son whose name was Solomon. And Solomon became the next king of Israel after the death of David (I Chronicles 28:5-7).

The mark of true forgiveness is illustrated in this story. Like love, true forgiveness does not keep a record of wrong. It promotes peace, not hatred; pardon instead of retaliation; clemency instead of punishment; vindication, as opposed to blame.

God opened a new chapter for David and his son Solomon, to establish the fact that when He forgives, He also forgets the sin meaning, when you forgive someone of any trespass, you must learn to forget.

CHAPTER TWELVE

THE MYSTERY OF THE NEW BIRTH IS A LIVING REALITY IN THE WORLD TODAY

The new birth in Christ is not just a theory, but an ordained fact given by heaven and established on the earth. Even though it is a mystery, its results are tangible. The aspects of the new birth are mysterious because they are not physical, but spiritual. They are not made by man, but fashioned by God. The new birth comes from above and not below.

Because of its nature, it can only be obtained on the basis of faith. Nicodemus, a religious leader of his day, asked the all-important question, as to how a man could be born again. Could he enter the second time into his mother's womb? Master Jesus explained that the new birth is not natural, but supernatural, and that Nicodemus must be born of water and of the Spirit (John 3:3-7).

A. I Am a Living Witness

I was born in 1955 in a village where we lacked electricity, hospitals/clinics, and doctors and nurses. My mother birthed me all alone, in the bush on our farm. I was told that only when I began to cry did my grandmother realize something was wrong and hastily went to help care for mama and me.

I grew up on that farm and later went to the village to live. While growing up there, I heard no mention of Jesus, the Savior of the world. At age 15, I moved to Monrovia, the capital city of Liberia, to have the privilege of enrolling into academic school. When I was 18 years old, I heard the Gospel of Jesus Christ for the first time. That night became a turning point in my life. God is worthy to be praised!

Beloved, when I mention being a living witness, I'm talking about the reality of the new birth and my deliverance from the kingdom of darkness. Prior to accepting Christ, I was the "bad village boy" who became a problem to everyone that crossed my path. I suffered immensely under the suppression of the devil. Satan made several attempts to destroy me, but to no avail. When Jesus came into my heart and took authority over my life, I experienced a complete change. I have become a new person, the results of which are demonstrated in my family, Church and community life. He that is Almighty had a glorious plan for my life. Jesus took away my sins and gave me His righteousness. Since then, this new birth I have received by His Word and His Spirit is still a reality in my life in 2015. Praise His name! Here are more wonderful true stories of God's deliverance:

1. On two separate occasions I was at the point of drowning in a very dangerous river. I did not become a victim because the invisible hand of God was upon me.

2. I was once hit with a five pound hose and could have died instantly. Again, I narrowly escaped death, because God had ordained me for salvation before the foundations of the world.

3. I once slept beside a witch that could have snatched my spirit-man through witchery. I thank God for His mighty angels that watched over me that night.

All of these occurrences in my life which took place before I confessed Christ, are indications that God chose and elected me for His good purpose. The Lord preserved and blessed me even before my tiny life began in my mother's womb. The evidences of God's hand on my life have become even clearer since my encounter with Christ.

My dear friend, If God could transform me, having been destructive and notorious, He can undoubtedly change you or anybody on the face of the earth. ***COME TO JESUS TODAY AND BE SAVED!***

B. My Family is a Witness

In Acts 16:31 the Bible says, ***"... Believe on the Lord Jesus Christ, and thou shalt be saved, and thy house."*** This passage of Scripture reminds me of the power of God in transforming the lives of my siblings and my parents as well.

In one of our towns in Liberia where we had travelled to carry the Gospel message, we were rejected, beaten, mysteriously shot at with lightning from the kingdom of darkness and bewitched with voodoo powers, with the intent to kill us. Also, it was unfortunate that some of the young ladies traveling along with us were raped, while the pastor in charge of the team suffered serious injury. In the end God powerfully manifested Himself – a large number of people received Christ in the subsequent weeks and months. Amazingly, among them were some of those who had so wickedly persecuted us. Hallelujah!

Several churches have been built in that very town and its surroundings since this incident; and the power of the Gospel continues to prevail, to the praise of His glory.

D. God is Saving People all Around the World Today

The wonders of the new birth began in Jerusalem with the 120 disciples (Acts 1:14-15). In chapter two after the preaching of Peter the apostle, there were added unto the Church three thousand souls. In chapter four, another five thousand were added. From then on, the Church grew to such extent that the believers became uncountable.

Christianity has grown in such magnitude that "there are 2.18 billion Christians of all ages around the world, representing nearly a third of the estimated 2010 global population of 6.9 billion," according to Pew Research Centers.

Indeed, the new birth is a mystery, attainable only by grace through faith. The same God that has saved my family and me, in addition to billions of people around the globe, can also save you today. He has selected you to become a member of His Holy Family, but the choice is yours. Just remember that **until you are saved, you are not safe.**

I charge you, therefore, in the authority of the mighty name of Jesus Christ, **TO *COME TO HIM TODAY. IF YOU ARE ALREADY SAVED, PLEASE RUN WITH THE GOSPEL TO OTHERS!***

GOD BLESS YOU!

CONCLUSION

In my final analysis of this book, let me remind you that there are vast differences between Christianity and all other religions.

A. Christianity offers life: spiritual, physical and eternal. Jesus said, "… I am come that they might have life, and that they might have it more abundantly" (John 10:10; John 3:16; 6:58).
B. Christianity offers complete forgiveness (Matthew 18:21-22, Luke 17:3, 4; 23:34).
C. Christianity assures its followers of peaceful rest in heaven when they leave this world (John 11:25-27; II Timothy 4:18; Philippians 3:20, 21).
D. Christianity provides overall peace and joy. Our captain, the Lord Jesus Christ said: "…My peace I give unto you: not as the world giveth…" (John 14:27; Hebrews 12:14; Romans 12:18).
E. The Christian religion is the giver of light. Jesus said: "I am the light of the world: he that followeth me shall not walk in darkness, but shall have the light of life" (John 8:12; I John 1:5-7).

I admonish you to choose this day whom you will serve; whether your money, your education, your fame or power. As for me and my house, we will serve the Lord Jesus Christ (Joshua 24:15). Today as you hear His voice, harden not your heart. Tomorrow is not promised to you. Your opportunity to know Him is now. Please consider reading these Scriptures:

1) **Romans 5: 8** – *"But God commendeth His love toward us, in that, while we were yet sinners, Christ died for us."*
2) **John 3:16** – *"For God so loved the world that he gave his only begotten Son, that whosoever believeth in Him should not perish, but have everlasting life."*
3) **Romans 3:23** – *"For all have sinned, and come short of the glory of God;"*
4) **Romans 6:23** – *"For the wages of sin is death; but the gift of God is eternal life through Jesus Christ our Lord."*
5) **Romans 10:9& 10** – *"That if thou shalt confess with thy mouth the Lord Jesus, and shalt believe in thine heart that God hath raised Him from the dead, thou shalt be saved. For with the heart man believeth unto righteousness; and with the mouth confession is made unto salvation."*

Remember, until ***you are saved, you are not safe.*** May God's glorious wealth of salvation become yours today, in the mighty name of JESUS CHRIST, Amen!

SUMMARY

This book is about understanding God's message of salvation, redemption, deliverance and reconciliation for all mankind, particularly for you as an individual whom God loves dearly. God designed the plan, the Son executed it by His death on the cross, and now the Holy Spirit is working it out on a daily basis to save you, if you do not know Christ.

In II Peter 3:9 the Bible says, " *The lord is not slack concerning His promise, as some men count slackness; but is longsuffering to us-ward, not willing that any should perish, but that all should come to repentance."*

Salvation, then, is mandatory. In this title, you will discover that salvation is not a natural phenomenon, but God giving life back to man. In addition to initial, progressive and future salvation, many other Biblical concepts and truths are packaged in this book. They are teachings that will inspire and save you. Friend, if you don't know what it really means to be born again, this book has the answer for you.

Despite the fact that God made His free gift available to all mankind more than 2000 years ago, He is patiently waiting for the lost to come to repentance. This is exemplary of His everlasting love for mankind.

If you are already a believer, you are the instrument of God for the salvation of the lost. Please do not let a day elapse without witnessing to someone about the Lord Jesus Christ, the Savior of the world.

GOD BLESS YOU!

REFERENCES

Bethany House Publishers. (1984). *The Expanded Vine's Expository Dictionary of New Testament Words.* Bethany House Publishers: Minneapolis, MN.

Guralnik, D. B. (1970). *2ndCollege Ed. Webster's New World Dictionary of the American Language.* The World Publishing Company: New York, Cleveland.

Evans, William. (1974). *The Great Doctrines of the Bible.* The Moody Bible Institute: Chicago, IL.

Hagin, K. E. (1997). *Welcome to God's Family: A foundational Guide for Spirit-filled Living.* Kenneth Hagin Ministries, Inc: Tulsa, OK.

Holman Bible Publishers. (2007). *KJV Super Giant Print Dictionary and Concordance. Holman Bible Publishers:* Nashville, TN.

Kenneth Hagin Ministries, Inc. (1985). *KJV Holy Bible: Rhema Study.* Kenneth Hagin Ministries, Inc: Tulsa, OK.

The Southwestern Company. (2006). *Vol. 2 The Volume Library.* The South Western/Great American Inc: Nashville, TN.

1. "Natural Law," International Encyclopedia of the Social Sciences, New York, 1968

2. Pew Research Centers, "Global Christianity – A Report on the Size and Distribution of the World's Christian Population" December 30, 2011, 6:30 p.m. https://m.brookline.wicked local.com/article/20111230/News/312309997. March 3, 2015, 8:30 p.m.

ABOUT THE AUTHOR

Pastor Anthony Flomo Blessed Tarnue hails from Lofa County in the West African Country of Liberia.

He accepted Christ on the streets of Monrovia, the capital city of his homeland, in November 1973. Brother Tarnue's walk with the Lord took a turning point in 1978 when he received the Lord's audible call and commission to proclaim the Good News of the Gospel of Jesus Christ – in a vision, the Holy Spirit opened his spiritual eyes to see a multitude of people that seemed to be perplexed, yet eagerly waiting in expectation for something.

Commonly known as the "street evangelist" in Liberia, Pastor Tarnue has been faithful to his calling to win the lost for Christ at all costs.

As founder and General Overseer of the International Free Pentecostal Church, Inc., Pastor Tarnue has been serving in the pastoral ministry for 36 years. His Church is headquartered in Philadelphia, USA, with several older branches in Montserrado, Lofa, Bomi and Margibi counties in Liberia, as well as in Eyeazu, Guinea, West Africa.

Pastor Tarnue began Biblical studies at the Monrovia Bible Training Institute, earning a diploma. He also holds a Bachelor of Arts Degree in Theology from the Carver Bible College in Paynesville, Liberia.

He presently resides in the USA, is married to his beautiful wife, Esther, and they are blessed with seven children.

Printed in the United States
By Bookmasters